A BARTHOLOMEW MAP & GUIDE

WALK CORK & KERRY

INCLUDING KILLARNEY
BY DAVID PERROTT AND JOSS LYNAM

G000018068

British Library Cataloguing in Publication Data
Perrott, David
    Walk Cork & Kerry.
    1. (County) Kerry. Visitors' guides 2. (County) Cork.
    Visitors' guides
    I. Title II. Lynam, Joss
    914'19 604824

ISBN 0–7028–0949–7

Published by Bartholomew, Duncan Street, Edinburgh EH9 1TA.
Printed by Bartholomew in Edinburgh, Scotland.

First Edition 1990

Produced for Bartholomew by
Perrott Cartographics, Darowen, Machynlleth, Powys SY20 8NS.

Typesetting by Perrott Cartographics and Litho Link Ltd.
Litho origination by Litho Link Ltd, Welshpool, Powys, SY21 8HJ.

The physical landscape of Ireland is changing all the time and
ownership of land is also subject to change. While every care has been
taken in the preparation of this guide, it should be noted that there is
no formal system of recognised rights of way in Ireland and, as a
result, the publishers and authors accept no responsibility whatsoever
for any loss, damage, injury or inconvenience sustained or caused as
a result of using this guide. Those who use the guide are reminded
that their personal safety and well-being are their own responsibility,
and are advised to heed advice and warnings. Walkers should check
locally if in any doubt and should always ensure that they take all
necessary clothing, equipment, maps, compass and food, and follow
advice regarding mountain safety (see page 8). They should also
adhere to The Country Code (see page 10).

All distances given within the walk instructions are approximations
in imperial measure, followed by the metric equivalent.

We gratefully acknowledge the assistance of Con Moriarty and
Gwynn Stephenson who, between them, are responsible for most of
the field work and route descriptions. We acknowledge the
contributions made by Belinda Baldock, Tom Finn and Marina
Baker, who also wrote descriptions.
We are also greatly indebted to Frank Donaldson, Senior Tourism
Officer of Cork/Kerry Tourism; Bill Gregor; Sean Ó Suilleabhain
and John Thuillier.

ISBN 0 7028 0949 7

CONTENTS

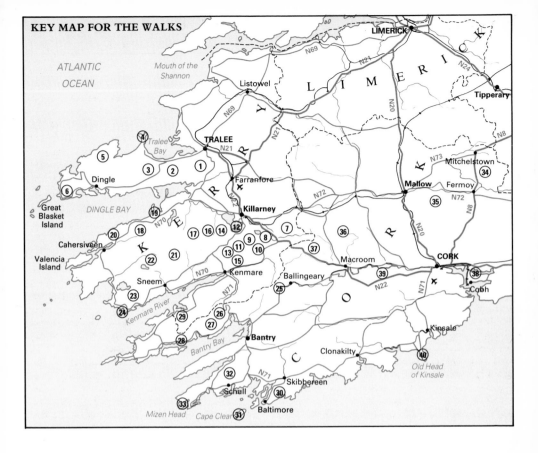

KEY MAP FOR THE WALKS

ATLANTIC
OCEAN

Mouth of the
Shannon

LIMERICK

Listowel

Tralee
Bay

TRALEE

Dingle

DINGLE BAY

Great
Blasket
Island

Cahersiveen

Valencia
Island

Sneem

Kenmare River

Bantry Bay

Mizen Head

Cape Clear

Baltimore

Schull

Skibbereen

Clonakilty

Old Head
of Kinsale

Kinsale

Cobh

CORK

Macroom

Ballingeary

Kenmare

Killarney

Farranfore

Mallow

Fermoy

Mitchelstown

Tipperary

LIMERICK

KERRY

CORK

Key to maps

Scale 1:48500

Scale 1:31600

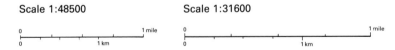

0   1 mile
0   1 km

0   1 mile
0   1 km

All maps are drawn on a north axis, ie, with north at the top

——— Road	❋ Viewpoint	Woods or forest
– – – Track or footpath	▲ Summit	Beach
– – – Route of walk	Slope or crags	
Ⓐ Description in text	553m Spot height in metres	Ⓟ Parking

WALKING IN CORK AND KERRY

South-west Ireland stretches four gnarled and calloused fingers out into the Atlantic, all of them offering interesting and exciting walks and most of them providing a wonderful combination of 'hills and sea'. Even the top of Ireland's highest mountain, Corrán Tuathail, 3409 ft (1039 m) is only 10 miles from Dingle Bay in the north, and the same distance from the Kenmare River (actually a fjord) in the south. For the walker, the great advantage of this situation is that quite short walks will often reveal magnificent distant views.

The country people of Kerry and west Cork are hardy farmers and fishermen who, on land or sea, have made a livelihood out of a harsh environment. They are a friendly people, who generally welcome strangers, and will appreciate a greeting and a few words of chat if you meet them on track or mountain.

1 THE SHAPING OF THE LAND

Cork and Kerry are formed largely of rocks of the Old Red Sandstone period, thrust up in the Hercynian mountain building. These thrust lines were north-south, resulting in the series of east-west ridges that form the four fingers, continuing eastwards a little less distinctly. At the time of the Hercynian movement, the sandstone was overlaid by Carboniferous limestone. This has been almost entirely eroded from the tops of the anticlines (folds in the strata), but remains in the valleys of east and south Cork, and below the sea in the rias (fjords) which separate the four fingers. Proceeding from east to west, the anticlines become higher and the synclines (troughs) deeper, culminating in the high mountains of Kerry. The highest mountains of all, the MacGillycuddy's Reeks, have been further heightened by a fault just to the north.

In the Tertiary period (relatively recent, in geological terms) all Ireland was beneath the sea, and covered in a layer of deposits which blanketed the whole country, leaving gentle slopes on which the rivers cut mainly north-south valleys. This resulted in the unexpected twists of the rivers of Cork – the Blackwater, the Lee and the Bandon – which flow peacefully west to east and then suddenly, breaching the hard sandstone ridges by impressive gorges, flow south to the sea. Originally they all flowed north-south, but as the softer, later, rocks and limestone eroded, the east-west valleys deepened, the pattern changed, and the present trellis-work of river valleys evolved.

The present shape of the mountains is the result of the last Ice Age. The last major ice sheet never quite reached down into Kerry, but the mountains of Kerry were high enough, in that cold climate, to have their own mountain glaciation. To this glaciation we owe most of the features of the mountains of Cork and Kerry. The glaciers gouged out steep-sided valleys and, in places, the rocks carried in the ice overdeepened the valley to leave the hollows which now contain lakes. Smaller side glaciers had less power to deepen their beds, and the retreat of the ice has left these side corries (hanging valleys) perched high above the main valley, often containing their own lakes. Where the glacier ended, it deposited its load of rocks as a terminal moraine. These crescent moraine ridges have also served to dam such lakes as Lough Leane. Sometimes the ice overfilled a valley, and overflowed across a ridge, cutting down as it overflowed. This is the probable origin of many of the passes of the region, such as the Gap of Dunloe. The higher summits were probably above the ice and resembled, on a small scale, the Alps of today, with their frost-shattered rocks, in contrast often with the ice-smoothed rock lower down. Most of the corries face north, or north east, which was presumably the colder side. Sometimes there are multiple lakes (as on the east of Brandon), and these are known as 'paternoster lakes', from their resemblance to the beads on a rosary. In the Dingle and Iveragh Peninsulas, the corries have generally cut back so far that only a sharp narrow ridge separates them from the next valley, but in the Beara Peninsula the valleys and corries generally fall from flat, boggy, and rather dull plateaux. Finally as the ice withdrew, it gouged out impressive channels like the Pass of Keimaneigh east of Gougane Barra.

Characteristically, the sandstone forms dark cliffs striped with horizontal bands of heather and rough grass but, in places, the grinding of the ice has produced very beautiful, rough, pale purple hogsbacks of rock, a delight to look at and to walk on. There has also been some volcanic activity, notably around Bennaunmore.

Further east, the effects of the ice are less marked, and the Boggeragh and Nagles Mountains are less rugged, though still bleak and bare. The valleys of limestone or softer shales, with the rock often overlain by glacial deposits, are broader and flatter, creating richer farmlands. Moving south and east, to Cork City and east Cork, this change becomes very marked; the pasture farms of the west give way to mixed tillage and pasture, farms get larger, and there is a general air of greater prosperity in the countryside. The backdrop of hills, too, is now frequently clothed in dark green forestry, almost to their summits.

2 LAND USE

The hill and moorland areas are extensively grazed by sheep. Off the hills, the main agricultural land use is dairy farming. Farms are mostly quite small, 30 to 60 acres (12 to 24 hectares), and to make such units viable, the farmers have set up co-operative creameries which have been very successful. These farms generally sell their calves for rearing elsewhere, and will often go in for pig-rearing as a sideline. They will also grow some oats and potatoes.

Further east, the pattern amongst the hills of north Cork hardly changes, except that there are a lot more conifer plantations (there are 63,000 acres [25,515 hectares] in the county, mostly in the north). However, in south and east Cork, on richer soils, there is a different way of life. Wheat, barley and sugar-beet are grown, and abundant fodder supplies mean that cattle can be reared through the winter,

and dairying is less important.

There are two other aspects of land use which will soon become very obvious to the walker. After the Great Famine of 1845-47 there was a huge population drop, and consequently a great reduction in the area actually farmed. On the open moorland you will often see the remains of old stone field boundaries and, even more noticeable, the patches where potatoes were grown. To obtain sufficient depth for the roots, the soil was scraped up into ridges, with the furrows between down almost to bare rock. They are called 'spade ridges' or 'lazy beds' and in many places the corrugated traces of them can be found high above modern tillage levels.

Recent European Community farm policies are also changing the moorlands. There are big subsidies for sheep fences which are now being strung across the hillsides, and for access roads which are being bulldozed into the mountains. Once the vegetation cover has been broken to make the road, erosion occurs rapidly, making ugly scars which get bigger, rather than smaller, with time.

3 A BRIEF HISTORY

There is little written history of the region before the coming of the Normans around 1100 AD. The earliest archaeological sites in the region date to the Bronze Age, probably in the last millenium BC. In the last centuries BC, the Celts, bringing iron weapons and tools, arrived and have left their mark over the whole island. In Cork and Kerry there are very many ancient 'raths' and 'duns', stone or earthen forts probably of Celtic origin, of which Staigue Fort is probably the finest example. In early Christian times, the bleak Kerry mountains and coast were favourite resorts of monks and anchorites. Of the many ruins of this time, in the form of simple drystone 'beehive' dwellings, the monastery on the bare rocky island of Skellig Michael, 8 miles (13 km) off the western end of the Iveragh Peninsula, is the most impressive, and is known internationally. The monastery ruins are situated on top of the rocky island, 600 steps above the small pier.

While it is sometimes hard to distinguish history from mythology, it is clear that there was a strong Munster kingdom during the first millenium AD, though its centre of gravity was further east, around

Cashel in Co Tipperary. It was from here that Brian Boru set out to become High King of all Ireland, and to defeat the Norsemen at Clontarf in 1014. These Norsemen had been raiding the Irish coasts for a couple of centuries before that, and not even the poor monks on Skellig Michael escaped their attention. They settled round the coast, and many Irish ports have a Norse origin; Cork might claim an older origin (its patron, Saint Finbar, is credited with building a church there in the 6th century), but it seems to have been mainly a Norse foundation, as was Youghal.

The Normans came to Ireland in 1169, and within 60 years had established themselves all over Cork and most of Kerry. However, the Irish chieftains fought back and, at the battle of Callan, near Kenmare in 1261, the MacCarthys and the O'Sullivans totally defeated the Norman FitzThomas Geraldines, ensuring that west Kerry and west Cork at least remained in Irish hands. From these troubled years date the enormous number of castles and towers to be found in the region. It was not just a time of fighting; the new rulers brought in Benedictines, Cistercians, Franciscans, and other orders, and many fine monasteries and friaries were built. They were also great church builders - St Mary's Collegiate church at Youghal dates from this period. In the 14th century the tide of conquest ebbed all over Ireland, until English rule was restricted to the Pale (area) around Dublin, and to the sea coast towns. Elsewhere, the old Gaelic chieftains, or the Norman lords who had intermarried with the Irish and become almost totally assimilated, ruled the country. The Earls of Desmond were effectively princes ruling over the four south-western counties, accepted by Norman and Irish alike, and increasingly estranged from their nominal rulers in Britain.

The Reformation brought a whole new dimension. To political disaffection was added religious differences, and Desmond and the other great Earls were the leaders of the battle against the new religion and the new centralising policies of the Tudor Monarchy. In the reign of Queen Elizabeth I, Munster rebelled three times under the Geraldine Earls of Desmond. Each time they were beaten and the countryside devastated. Most of the Desmonds were executed. After the collapse of the rebellion in 1583 a great plantation scheme for much of Munster was planned, and such famous names as Sir Walter Raleigh, the explorer, and Edmund Spenser, the poet, received large grants. However, very few settlers arrived and those that had come fled the next rebellion in 1598. The last kick of independent Ireland in Munster was at Kinsale in 1601. A Spanish invasion force was besieged there by the English, and an Irish army marched all the way from Donegal to relieve the Spaniards, only to be defeated and scattered by an English army under Lord Mountjoy. It was at this time that the famous march of O'Sullivan Beare took place, when he moved with his whole clan from Dunboy in the Beara Peninsula to Leitrim; harried all the way by the English, only a handful reached their destination.

The 16th century saw the takeover of all the richer lands by protestant landowners. Raleigh sold his 42,000 acres (1701 hectares) to the enterprising Richard Boyle, later Earl of Cork. Boyle introduced English settlers, developed industry, fostered old towns, and founded new ones. Bandon is his creation – a bastion against the Gaelic lands to the west. Many fine houses were built by these landowners in the succeeding centuries – Bantry House, home of the Earls of Bantry, is a good example. After the Act of Union in 1800, when Ireland became part of the United Kingdom, Munster landowners, like their confrères elsewhere in Ireland, found it more and more difficult to maintain their properties. Many were absentees who tried to extort higher rents than the land could pay. The Great Famine of 1845-47 changed the scene utterly. Around this time the population of Ireland dropped by 2 million from its previous 8.5 million. Some of the old roads followed on the walks in this book are 'famine roads', built as relief works to help the starving landless labourers. Munster lost 23.5% of its inhabitants, and the decline continued until very recently. In the latter half of the 19th century many impoverished estates were sold to their tenants with the help of cheap state loans.

The best-known Kerryman in the 19th century was undoubtedly Daniel O'Connell, 'The Liberator', who lived in Derrynane (see Walk 24) at the tip of the Iveragh Peninsula. In 1829 he achieved Catholic Emancipation when he was elected MP for Co Clare, and was grudgingly allowed into the House of Commons, but his later campaign to reverse the Act of Union failed, dying out when the Famine of 1845-47 concentrated peoples' minds on the matter of physical survival.

The present century brought the War of Independence, followed by the Civil War between those who accepted the 'Irish Free State' as a British dominion, and those who held out for an independent republic. The strife in Cork and Kerry was particularly bitter – Michael Collins, leader of the Free State Army, was ambushed and killed at Bealnablath, north of Bandon.

Since independence the region has had a chequered prosperity; tourism has thrived – Killarney is the most popular tourist centre in Ireland – but industrial development has been spasmodic. Big employers, such as Ford, have come and gone, and the much-heralded Bantry Oil Terminal went up in smoke. Agriculture, at least, has thrived, since entering the European Economic Community.

4 RIGHTS OF WAY

There is no system of recognised rights of way such as is found in Britain, although there is a close network of by-roads, green tracks, mass paths, and other old tracks which are traditionally used by the public. Most Irish farmers have no objection to walkers crossing their land – provided they observe The Country Code – but, in compiling this selection of 40 walks, we have taken into account the fact that farmers are understandably reluctant to see published routes across their land, resulting in heavy usage. Many farmers feel this way in the area covered by the guide and, particularly in the richer, more populous land of east Cork.

Almost all of the walking is on countryside tracks and open ground but, in order to avoid inconvenience to farmers, some of the walks include tarmac sections where necessary. These are pleasant and easier to follow than directions through fields, as well as being more considerate to those who make their living from the land. The only area where it is possible to wander freely is on the open hills and, even there, you must remember that someone is using those same hills to scrape a difficult livelihood.

Whether you are following tracks, or walking on the hills, farmers **will not welcome your dog if it is not on a lead**. There have been too many instances of sheep worrying by dogs for them to be allowed to run free. So please keep your dog on a lead or, preferably, don't bring it with you on a walk over open land. A dog found worrying sheep – and 'worrying' is interpreted fairly widely – may legally be shot. Several walks (**13 & 15**, for example) pass through hills where red deer roam – **dogs should not accompany you in these areas at all**, on or off the lead.

Every walk in this guide has been checked very thoroughly and carefully to ensure that there will be no access problems for walkers. However, situations can change, such as when land is sold, and we recommend that you heed any warning notices or advice given locally.

5 MAPS

While each walk is accompanied by its own map, more general maps of the area are useful for getting your bearings. The Irish Ordnance Survey 1:250,000 (approx 0.25 inch to 1 mile) sheet 4 (South), gives useful information.

6 SAFETY

The walks in this guide are intended for the enjoyment of all. Many are on tracks and paths, and an accident is most unlikely. Others do go into the hills, and readers are reminded that they should appreciate that walking in hills has always a slight element of risk. They should understand that climbing Corrán Tuathail (Walk **17**) is quite a different proposition from walking round Fota Island (Walk **38**), and they should plan accordingly.

On high level walks in particular, safety precautions should be taken before you depart. None of the hill walks should be undertaken unless the party is clothed and equipped against possible sudden bad weather (see below), and unless some member of the party can read a map and use a compass in case of difficulty. Never start a high level walk in bad weather, and always allow for sudden changes. Remember that you can easily get lost in the mist on a mountain top when the valleys below are clear and warm. Take note of prominent landmarks on the way up so that you can find your way down easily. A first-aid kit, a torch and some high energy food (chocolate and fruit bars, for example) and drink are also essential, carried in a lightweight rucksack.

Proper walking boots, a waterproof anorak, and preferably waterproof over-trousers, are essential for the high level walks, and are strongly recommended for any walk in open country. Several layers of clothing are preferable to one heavy jacket or sweater, so that you can always maintain a comfortable temperature. Avoid wearing jeans (which are very uncomfortable when soaked) and carry a pair of trousers (tracksuit trousers are ideal) if you are wearing shorts. A warm hat and gloves are invaluable.

Plan your walks allowing plenty of time for stops to enjoy the views, and picnics. Walk with a steady rhythm, at the pace of the slowest member of the party. On the high walks especially, you must ensure that the walking group does not split up. Take short steps on uneven ground, taking care not to dislodge stones onto those below. Do not attempt to cross streams in spate – if in doubt, turn back. Unless you are *highly* experienced, you should never venture into the hills alone. In the event of an accident, should you or one of your party be able to reach a telephone, the appropriate rescue organisation, be it an ambulance or a Mountain Rescue Team, can be summoned by dialling 999.

7 WEATHER

Ireland has a reputation, which is not really justified, for rain. It lies in the path of all the depressions that whirl eastwards across the Atlantic, and the west coast mountains, forcing the clouds upwards till they shed their loads of water vapour, do get plenty of rain. Nevertheless, perhaps the prime characteristic of Irish weather is its changeability. In a few minutes the clouds will lift to brilliant sunshine, the rain-soaked air creating crystal-clear views with wonderful colours. Equally, a fine sunny day may turn quickly to rain! So the walker should not be put off by a wet morning (unless planning a high level walk), nor tempted by a brilliant sunny dawn to leave his rain gear behind. Walkers should remember that temperature decreases by up to 3°C per 1000 feet (300 m), and windspeeds at 3000 feet

(914 m) may easily be 2.5 times what they are at sea level.

Generally the best month in Ireland for sunshine is May, and this is especially true of the south-west. June and July are also good, though probably wetter than May. August is definitely wet, but September and October can often be very beautiful months. November and December are bad months for walking anywhere in the Northern Hemisphere; January can give fine crisp days, February tends to be wet, but March frequently gives fine though coldish weather, and April is grand between the showers. The essence of Irish weather is changeability, so don't rely on the good, or be unduly discouraged by the bad.

A recorded weather forecast for the area covered by this book can be obtained by telephoning 021-964600.

8 ACCOMMODATION

Cork and Kerry are very much tourist areas and accommodation of all types is very easy to find. Bord Fáilte Eireann, the Irish Tourist Board, publishes annual guides to all registered and approved accommodation, from Grade A hotels to farmhouses, with details of facilities available, and charges. These can be bought in any Irish Tourism Office and are well worth their modest cost. An Oige, the Irish Youth Hostel Association, also publishes an annual booklet on their hostels. Bord Fáilte and Cork-Kerry Tourism, the Regional Tourism Organisation, can supply much useful information about all aspects of a visit to the region.

Useful addresses:
Bord Fáilte Eireann
Baggot Street Bridge, Dublin 2. Tel 01-765871.
150 New Bond Street, London W1Y 0AQ. Tel 01-4933201.
Cork-Kerry Tourism Offices
Tourism House, Grand Parade, Cork. Tel 021-273251.
Town Hall, Killarney, Co Kerry. Tel 064-31633.
Main Street, Skibbereen, Co Cork. Tel 028-21766.
An Oige (IYHA)
39 Mountjoy Square, Dublin 1. Tel 01-363111.

9 TRANSPORT

There are international air services to Shannon, Cork and Farranfore (Killarney), and frequent rail services to Cork, Killarney and Tralee.

There are car ferry services to Cork from both Britain and France, and also very frequent car ferry services from both these countries to Rosslare, some 130 miles (209 km) from Cork and 170 miles (274 km) from Killarney.

Public transport within the area is poor. Bus services are infrequent, particularly in Kerry. For such as exist, a timetable can be obtained from **Bus Eireann** The Broadstone, Dublin 7.

In practice, private transport is about the only feasible method of getting to most of the walks we describe. While a car, even a hired car, is the most comfortable solution, a bicycle is an alternative which should be considered; it is possible to hire bicycles in the main towns in the region.

10 THE COUNTRY CODE

Enjoy the countryside and respect its life and work.
Guard against all risk of fire.
Leave gates as you find them.
Keep your dogs under close control.
Keep to public paths across farmland.
Use gates and stiles to cross fences, hedges and walls.
Leave livestock, crops and machinery alone.
Take your litter home.
Help to keep all water clean.
Protect wildlife, plants and trees.
Take special care on country roads.
Make no unnecessary noise.

11 NATURAL HISTORY

While the acid soils of west Cork and Kerry discourage some plants, and the strong west winds from the Atlantic stunt growth in exposed places, the presence of the Gulf Stream just off the west coast produces a mild climate which encourages abundant vegetation and fine trees in sheltered places.

In the Killarney National Park and the Glengarriff State Forest there are probably the most extensive natural woodlands remaining in Ireland. On the lower mountain slopes are native oakwoods, dominated by the Sessile Oak *(Quercus petraea)*, with holly and other evergreens in the understorey. Yew trees will be found, and birches are also common, as are rowans (mountain ash), found a little higher. None of these are real rarities, but both Killarney and Gougane Barra (see Walk **25**) can boast of the unusual strawberry tree *(Arbutus unedo)*. The most obvious shrubs are fuchsia, gorse and rhododendron. The bright yellow flower masses of gorse seem to put in an appearance somewhere in every month of the year, and fuchsia, with its beautiful red dangling blooms lends an almost Mediterranean feel to the countryside. Unfortunately, the mild climate has helped the epidemic growth of the rhododendron, which, introduced from the Himalaya in the last century, is now spreading out of control, and has become a pest around Killarney. Its gnarled roots are almost impossible to dig up, and its contorted branches are almost impassible. The mild climate also promotes the growth of mosses and ferns, many of which will be found growing on the branches and trunks of trees.

Besides Killarney, there are other wooded areas, but in most of them the State has been at work, and there is either a mixture of natural woodland and planted conifers, or complete cover of conifers. There has been much insensitive planting, with harsh boundaries and little variety of species, but the State's Open Forest policy, which permits us to walk freely in these forests, is to be commended.

On the open, higher ground, the most common plants are heather and its related species, and mountain grasses and sedges. The boggy areas are dominated by sphagnum mosses with tufts of molinia, scirpus, or other tough grasses. Bog cotton, *(Eriophorum angustifolium)* with its white cottony heads is common, as is the yellow asphodel *(Narthecium ossifragum)*. Less obvious, but as widespread, are the pale purple flowers of the butterworts *(Pinguicula sp)*, and the sticky red-haired leaves of the sundew *(Drosera rotundifolia)*. These plants have solved the problem of the poor nutritive value of the acid soils by turning carniverous, and trapping small flies.

Most of the other species usually found on acid

hillsides are present, but the south west has a speciality of its own – the Lusitanian plants, a species found only in south and west Ireland and in the Iberian peninsula. Examples are St Patrick's Cabbage *(Saxifraga spathularis)*, Irish Spurge *(Euphorbia hyberna)*, and the Giant Butterwort *(P. grandiflora)*, whose magnificent flowers are over 0.75 inch (20 mm) across.

The mountain tops are mostly too bare and windswept for all but the hardiest vegetation – club mosses, lichens, and a few ground-hugging plants. East and south Cork, except for the hill areas, are a great contrast, for this is a rich agricultural zone of mixed farming, and the wild flora is not of much interest.

The range of mammals in the area is small. Of pre-eminent interest are the red deer (see Torc, Walk **13** and The Old Kenmare Road, Walk **15**); there are also introduced Japanese sika deer and feral goats, perhaps originally of domestic origin (look out for goats on Mangerton, Walk **11**). There are plenty of hares, and rabbits are recovering fast from the myxomatosis epidemic; there are foxes, stoats, hedgehogs and shrews. Red squirrels are also to be found near the Old Kenmare Road (Walk **15**). In the lower areas there are badgers, but they are increasingly rare as they are being killed off in the unconfirmed belief that they transmit tuberculosis to domestic cattle.

The area is so rich in birdlife that only a few selected species can be mentioned here. Birds of prey are represented by the merlin, the kestrel and the peregrine – this last seems to be recovering from its near extinction by DDT and to be spreading slowly, though it is still an endangered species. Its wild screeches will soon let you know if you go anywhere near its eyrie! Among the Corvidae, the raven is to be found on most crags, the carrion crow is ubiquitous, and the chough will be found on sea-cliffs and the heights. On moorland you will hear, even if you do not see, the singing skylarks, along with grouse, snipe and, perhaps commonest of all, the meadow pipit. In a mountain stream, if you are fortunate, you may see a dipper. Around the lakes there are heron and, in winter, the magnificent Whooper Swan arrives. A small colony of Greenland White Fronted Geese winters near Killarney.

12 OGHAM SCRIPT

You will see examples of Ogham insriptions on several of the walks in this guide. The letters employed are based on a simple plan, but one which is exceedingly cumbrous in execution. Short strokes are made on either side of a line, or crossing it either diagonally or at right angles. The line in the surviving inscriptions is almost always one edge of a standing stone, making them very difficult to decipher. The inscriptions are generally restricted to the name of the owner or erector of the stone.

The script flourished from the 4th to the 7th centuries, and is almost exclusively Irish. At least 300 examples are known in Ireland, with a few in Scotland, Wales and the Cornish peninsula, doubtless the work of Irish emigrants, since the script is quite unknown on Continental Europe. Ogham even survived in remote areas of Ireland until the last century. R L Praeger quotes the amusing story of a farmer who was prosecuted for not having his name on his cart, and indignantly pointed out that it *was* there – in Ogham!

AOU E I HDT C Q BL F S NMGNG Z R

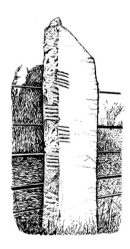

An Ogham stone at Dunloe, Co Kerry.

11

13 PLACE NAMES AND THE IRISH LANGUAGE

The first language in most parts of Cork and Kerry is English, but there are 'Gaeltacht' areas where Irish is spoken as a first language; these are the Dingle Peninsula (see Walks 5 & 6), Ballyvourney, Coolea, Ballingeary, and Cape Clear Island (see Walk 31). Even in the Gaeltacht, everyone can speak and understand English.

Most towns have both an Irish and an English name and, generally, it is not too difficult to recognise the Irish version. The names of places in the countryside are nearly all of Irish origin, but were transliterated by English-speaking surveyors in the 19th century, in such a fashion that it is now sometimes impossible to guess at the original Irish version. At the time most country people were Irish-speaking only, and the surveyors had not only to transliterate the name, they had to make their informants understand which feature they wanted the name for. That they were unsuccessful sometimes is borne out by the number of mountains whose names begin with 'Coum', cognate with Welsh 'cwm' and English 'coomb', meaning a valley. The transliteration has created a further difficulty in that there is no generally accepted spelling for some place names. For instance 'Carrauntoohil' will be found in a variety of spellings – we have used Corrán Tuathail, the Irish version, as the least contentious. In general, wherever possible, we have tried to use names as they are most commonly known. In the text we often give the generally accepted English meanings for place names in Irish, but there are often one, or even two, dissenting opinions.

The following is a list of Irish words which you will often see used in place names. There are two major linguistic problems with these. Firstly, how to pronounce words which present a forest of unusual consonant combinations with an 'h' (séamhú), such as dh, bh, mh, th, gh, etc. The effect of the 'h' is to soften the consonant so that 'mh' is 'v', 'bh' is 'v' or 'w', 'th' is 'h', and the others are often silent. The symbol (´), looking like a French acute accent, is called a fada, and lengthens the vowel.

Secondly, words are given in the nominative case,

but in the Irish language, when nouns are used in a qualifying sense, the spelling of the genitive may change, as in the following examples:
Knocknadobar is Cnoc na dTobar, the Hill of the Wells. (Tobar is the nominative, dTobar the genitive).

Annamoe is Ath na mBo, the Ford of the Cows. (Bó is the nominative, mBó is the genitive – the m silences the B).

Abha, abhain (ow, owen)	river
Achadh (agha, augh)	field
Aill, faill	cliff
Alt	height, or side of glen
Ard	height, promontory
Ath	ford
Baile (bally)	village, town
Bán (bawn, baun)	white
Barr	top
Beag (beg)	small
Bealach (ballagh)	pass
Beann (ben)	peak
Bearna (barna)	gap
Beith (beigh)	birch tree
Bignian (binnian)	little peak
Bó	cow
Bóthar (boher)	road
Bothairín (bohereen)	lane
Breac (brack)	speckled
Brí (bree, bray)	hill
Buaille (booley)	summer pasture (for transhumance)
Bun	river mouth
Buí	yellow
Carn	cairn
Carraig (carrick)	a rock
Cathair (caher)	stone fort
Ceann (ken)	head (of a bay)
Ceathramhadh	quarter of land
Cill	church
Clár	plain, board
Cloch	stone
Clochóg	stepping stone
Cluain (cloon)	meadow
Cnoc (crock, knock)	hill
Coill (kyle, kill)	wood
Coire	corrie, cauldron
Cor	rounded hill
Corrán (carraun)	serrated mountain (sickle)

Cruach	steep hill
Cúm (coum)	corrie
Dearg	red
Doire (derry)	oak wood
Druim	ridge
Dubh (duff, doo)	black
Dún	fort, castle
Eas (ass)	waterfall
Eisc (esk)	steep, rocky gully
Fionn (fin)	fair, clear
Fraoch (freagh)	heath, heather
Gabhar (gower)	goat
Gaoith (gwee)	wind
Glas	green
Glais	streamlet
Gleann	glen
Gorm	blue
Gort	field (tilled)
Inbhear (inver)	river mouth
Inis	island
Lágh (law)	hill
Leacán (lackan)	hillside
Leacht	large heap of stones
Leitir (letter)	wet hillside
Liath (lea)	grey
Loch (lough)	lake, sea inlet
Lug	mountain hollow
Machaire (maghera)	plain
Mael, maol (mweel)	bare hill
Mór (more)	big, great
Mám, madhm (maum)	pass
Más	long low hill
Mullach	summit
Oilean	island
Poll	hole, pond
Riabhach	grey
Rinn	headland
Rua, ruadh	red
Scairbh (scarriff)	shallow ford
Scealp	rocky cleft
Sceilg (skellig)	rock
Sean	old
Sescenn (seskin)	marsh
Sidh (shee)	fairy, fairy hill
Sliabh (slieve)	hill, mountain
Slidhe (slee)	road
Spinc	pointed pinnacle
Sron	nose-like feature
Sruth, -air, -ań	stream
Stuaic (stook)	pointed pinnacle
Sui, suidhe (see)	seat
Taobh (tieve)	hillside
Teampull	church
Tír	land, territory
Teach	house
Tobar	well
Torc	wild boar
Tulach	little hill

Walk 1

KNOCKMOYLE AND SCOTIA'S GRAVE

6.5 miles (10.5 km) Easy – but not suitable after heavy rain

South and west of Tralee, the chief town of Co Kerry, lies the long ridge of the Slieve Mish (Sliabh Meissi, mountain of the phantoms). These are sandstone mountains, the attractions of which have been neglected in favour of Mount Brandon to the west and the MacGillycuddy's Reeks to the south. This route is conveniently close to Tralee and, without being strenuous, gives the walker a good sample of the Slieve Mish, and some splendid views. At first this route takes you onto the lesser summits of old red sandstone which form the Slieve Mish Mountains. There are good views throughout, at first south over the limestone plain of mid-Kerry to the majestic MacGillycuddy's Reeks, and later north over the Vale of Tralee and Tralee Bay. Towards the end of the walk, the route passes Queen Scotia's grave and finishes with a pleasant passage through a small wooded area. The end of the walk also includes three fords and so, even though the route could be reversed, it is perhaps wiser to follow the suggested direction. Then if you do get wet feet, this need only be endured for a short while!

A Directly to the south, you can see Killarney's Lough Leane and the twin peaks of Beenkeragh and Corrán Tuathail (see Walk **17**) towering over the other mountains of the MacGillycuddy's Reeks. To the south-west, there are views over Castlemaine Harbour, Rossbeigh Strand (see Walk **19**), Inch Strand and out into Dingle Bay.

B The mast here supports a dish used to reflect the microwave telephone link between Limerick and Tralee. It is referred to locally as the 'Iron Man'.

C To the north can be seen the town of Tralee, famous for the Rose of Tralee Festival. For a week at the end of August, the town bulges with visitors. Prospective Roses from all over Ireland, and from as far away as the United States in one direction and New Zealand in the other, enter the beauty competition, the winner being crowned 'Rose of Tralee' for a year. But the competition is only a part of the gaiety. There is music and singing and dancing and, needless to say, a lot of drinking. West of the town you can see the line of the old canal, now derelict, which linked Tralee with the sea beyond Blennerville. If the day is clear, you will also be able to see the restored windmill at Blennerville. Looking north-west across the sandspit known as Derrymore Island and Tralee Bay you can see the deep water pier at Fenit. This is one of the most important fishery harbours in Kerry.

D Just before the first ford crossing, where the stream approaches the path on the right, there is a large stone slab, supposedly marking the grave of Queen Scotia. The Queen is traditionally believed to have been the daughter of a Pharoah, who died in battle on the Slieve Mish, in the 17th century BC. The edge of the stone may have been engraved with an Ogham inscription (see page 11), but this has been obliterated with carved names and initials.

Over

KNOCKMOYLE AND SCOTIA'S GRAVE

Continued

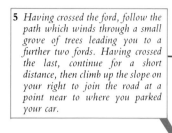

5 *Having crossed the ford, follow the path which winds through a small grove of trees leading you to a further two fords. Having crossed the last, continue for a short distance, then climb up the slope on your right to join the road at a point near to where you parked your car.*

4 *As you walk down by the course of the stream, a bog road can be seen to the right. Follow this for a while, then, having passed a small tributary of the Finglass Stream, drop down the slope, to the first of three fords.*

3 *Turn right at the summit to walk back parallel to your original route until you reach the small saddle you passed after leaving Knockmoyle. Now veer left to join a small stream flowing from the direction of the summit.*

1 *From the town of Tralee take the Ballyard Road. This starts at the crossroads near where the Tralee Canal begins. Follow the road to a T junction where you turn left and then right at the minor crossroads. Continue for 0.5 mile (0.8 km) until a small road is seen on the left. Park your car here.*
Walk up the road for about 1.5 miles (2.4 km) to the road's high point east of Knockmoyle.

2 *Turn right off the road and walk (due west) over open ground to the summit of Knockmoyle. From here veer a little to the left, and then to the right, to walk up the spur to the 1814 ft (553 m) peak ahead. As you reach the summit, the reflector mast comes into view.*

To Tralee

0   1 mile
0   1 km

Ⓟ

Ⓓ

Scotia's Grave

▲ Knockmichael Mountain

Ⓒ

553m ▲

Ⓑ

424m Knockmoyle

Ⓐ

15

Walk 2

CAHERCONREE

3 miles (4.8 km) Easy/Moderate

This walk visits the prehistoric inland promontory fort of Caherconree, and the mountain of the same name. There are breathtaking views of Brandon Bay, the Maharees (see Walk **4**) and Tralee Bay to the north and Dingle Bay, Castlemaine Harbour, the MacGillycuddy's Reeks and Killarney's lower lake to the south and south-east.

3 *Keeping the crags to your left, veer to the right to ascend to the summit of Caherconree at 2715 ft (828 m). Descend by the same route.*

1 *From Tralee, drive for 9 miles (14.5 km) along the T68 Dingle road, passing the villages of Blennerville and Derrymore. On the approach to the village of Camp, a signpost indicates a left turn towards Caherconree. Follow this road for 2.5 miles (4 km) until you can see the bottom of a very steep section of the road directly ahead. Caherconree is the high summit to your left. Park your car carefully on the roadside near a board marking the start of this walk.*
Walk towards the mountain, following the marker posts, over some wet ground, and then climb to the saddle between Caherbla and Caherconree.

To Camp

Caherconree
828m

Beheenagh

Caherbla

2 *Now veer to the left (north), climbing to 2,000 ft (610 m) on the south-west spur of Caherconree. Pause here to explore the ancient fort.*

A The Fort consists of a wall 350 ft (107 m) long, and 14 ft (4.3 m) thick, which cuts off a tongue of land 2000 ft (610 m) above sea level. There is a shallow ditch outside the wall and remnants of terraces inside the wall. The original entrance may have been 90 ft (27 m) from the north end and small square structures appear inside the wall at this point. Watch out for ravens as they ride the updraughts along the cliffs to your north-west. In folklore the fort was built by Cu Rai – a magical figure who carried off Cu Chulainn's girlfriend Blathnaid. However, Blathnaid helped Cu Chulainn get his revenge by telling him when the magically defended fort could be taken by force. Turning a stream white by pouring milk into it was the sign which, when seen, signalled to the awaiting Cu Chulainn that the time was right to attack and destroy the fort. This he did, and slew Cu Rai.

B There are spectacular views from this summit on a clear day. To the north-west, the sweep of Brandon Bay ends in the Maharees, whose sandy arm separates it from Tralee Bay. Looking due north across the Bay, look for the deep water pier at Fenit. Directly south is Castlemaine Harbour with the fine strands of Inch and Rossbeigh (see Walk **19**) separating it from Dingle Bay. Turning to the south-west, the majestic MacGillycuddy's Reeks can be seen towering over the lowland around Killorglin and Killarney's Lough Leane.

GLANNAGALT

6.5 miles (10.5 km) Easy

This walk runs through a sparsely populated sheep farming district, mostly on quiet country roads. Although it attains a height of 700 feet (213 m) the ascent is gradual. The area is rich in Megalithic monuments but, regrettably, there is no public right of access to some of them and they are best seen from the road. At all times the walker has fine views of mountains, valleys and the sea.

6 *After 500 yards (457 m) turn left at the creamery and then, shortly, right to return to Kilgobban Church, which is visible 0.5 mile (0.8 km) ahead.*

5 *At a crossroads turn sharply left. Keep on the tarmac road as it bends right and reaches a T junction about 1 mile (1.6 km) further on. Turn right here.*

4 *Turn right at the road. Walk for 50 yards (46 m) and cross the old railway bridge on the left. Carry on down the glen on a grassy road.*

1 *Start the walk at Kilgobban Church. To reach it take the Dingle Road (T68) from Tralee. After 9.5 miles (15.3 km), at Camp Junction, keep straight on in the direction of Brandon. After 0.5 mile (0.8 km) turn right at a telephone kiosk. The church is 0.5 mile (0.8 km) down this road. Park near it.*
Walk south towards the mountains. Cross a road, continue uphill and cross a second road. Go straight ahead with the slated Roman Catholic church on the left.

2 *Turn right when you reach a crossroads. There is a Dingle Way direction post here. Ahead is a steep fuchsia-lined bog road overlooking the valley of the Finglas River. Follow this.*

3 *Maumnahaltora is the highest point of this walk. At a T junction turn right and go downhill to reach the road, ignoring the Dingle Way markers.*

Map labels: Tralee Bay, Kilgobban Church, To Tralee, Camp, Faisi's Grave, Corrin, Maumnahaltora, Knockbrack, Gleann na nGealt, Course of Tralee & Dingle Railway, A, B, C, D, E, F

A A large flat stone lying in a field to the left of the road is known as Faisi's Grave. It bears a clear inscription in Ogham script (see page 11). In local mythology this is the burial place of Princess Fas, who was supposedly slain in a battle near here, along with Scotia, the daughter of a Pharoah and widow of Mil, who was once the leader of the prehistoric Gaelic invaders of Ireland.

B Caherconree is a well preserved promontory fort. It is clearly visible at the southern edge of the mountain range across the valley (see Walk 2).

C Maumnahaltora is the site of Megalithic wedge tombs and holy wells.

D Stretching westward is a large area of blanket bog known as Slieve. It is still worked for the harvesting of fuel.

E This is the route of the Tralee and Dingle narrow-gauge railway, which served the peninsula from 1891 to 1953. One of its engines may now be seen at Blennerville.

F Gleann na nGealt means 'Glen of the Mad People'. According to tradition the insane sought relief from their affliction in this lovely valley.

MAHAREES

5.5 miles (8.8 km) Easy

The prominent spur of land jutting northwards between Tralee Bay and Brandon Bay, and the rocky islands in its vicinity, are collectively known as the Maharees. Though devoid of any significant vegetation and exposed to salt winds on all sides this is an area of particular charm and interest. The scenery is splendid; bathing is safe and there are many archaeological remains. Bird life is very plentiful – especially in winter.

5 *Leave the pier on the tarmac road for Fahamore. Then **EITHER** a few yards beyond the village climb over the boulders on the right and turn left along the beach **OR** continue along the road to the end of the walk.*

4 *Go through Kilshannig village, leave the roadway and continue on the crescent beach. The path is now at the edge of a low shale cliff. It may be necessary to cover the last few hundred yards to Scraggane Pier on the rocky shore.*

6 *Houses are seen on the left behind the dunes. 500 yards (457 m) beyond these houses a gap in the sandhills framing an electricity pole indicates the short sandy lane and the end of the walk.*

1 *To reach the start of this walk, leave Tralee on the T68 and go to Castlegregory. Pass through the village in the direction of Fahamore. Just beyond the caravan parks is a wide flat expanse of dune land. About mid way on the road through here, on the left, is a 'No Dumping' sign near a short sandy lane. Park here, considerately. Cross the road and go over the grassy plain for 0.5 mile (0.8 km), towards a cow barn.*

3 *On the left is a slated house with flat-roofed additions. Stay close to the shore here, rounding Kilshannig Point and picking up a narrow path to seaward of a stone wall.*

2 *Reach the beach to the right of the cow barn. Turn left and walk on the foreshore and seashore for about 1 mile (1.6 km) towards the headland.*

A The ruined church at Kilshannig dates from about the 16th century and is dedicated to St Senach. Note the cross slab inside.

B The cone-shaped rock visible some 4 miles (6.4 km) offshore is Mucklagh. It rises to a height of 96 feet (29 m) and is completely barren. Landing is not normally possible.

C The Maharee Islands are sometimes called the 'Seven Hogs'. Illauntannig is the largest of the group and was inhabited until the 1950s. It contains extensive remains of early Christian settlements.

D Scraggane Pier is the home of the tiny local fishing fleet and berthing place for the traditional black curraghs.

MOUNT BRANDON VIA THE SAINTS ROAD

7 miles (11.3 km) Strenuous (see page 8)

0 _____ 1 mile
0 _____ 1 km

Mount Brandon, situated on the verge of the Atlantic on the Dingle Peninsula, is 3117 ft (950 m) high. The views from the summit are breathtaking and well worth the effort of the walk to the top which, starting virtually at sea level, is one of the longest in Ireland. Brandon is often termed a 'wet mountain', since it is regularly draped in cloud, so be sure to choose a fine day for this walk. In poor visibility it is possible to stray off the course of the faint track.

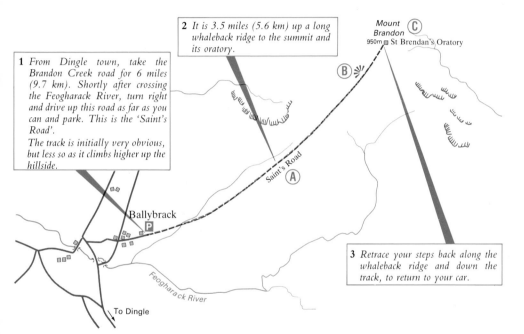

1 *From Dingle town, take the Brandon Creek road for 6 miles (9.7 km). Shortly after crossing the Feogharack River, turn right and drive up this road as far as you can and park. This is the 'Saint's Road'.*
The track is initially very obvious, but less so as it climbs higher up the hillside.

2 *It is 3.5 miles (5.6 km) up a long whaleback ridge to the summit and its oratory.*

Mount Brandon 950m □ St Brendan's Oratory ⓒ

ⓑ

Saint's Road ⓐ

Ballybrack Ⓟ

3 *Retrace your steps back along the whaleback ridge and down the track, to return to your car.*

Feogharack River

To Dingle

A Although many believe Brandon to be named after the early Irish missionary Saint Brendan, it is generally accepted that its name is derived from an earlier Irish voyager, Bran. St. Brendan is however associated with the mountain and the whole area around it. He reputedly spent long spells in the summit oratory in prayer, particularly prior to his famous voyage in or around 550 AD – when he supposedly discovered America.

B From the slopes of Brandon, the view westwards is dominated by the Blasket Island group. The largest of these, An Blascaod Mor, was inhabited up to 1953. From this last generation of islanders, three emerged as great writers. Writing in their native tongue, Peig Sayers, Thomas O'Criothan and Muiris O'Sulleabhain wrote of their lives as islanders in works that have been internationally acclaimed.

C Since earliest Christian times mass has been celebrated on the summit of Mount Brandon, with an astonishing 20,000 people attending on 28th June 1868, in the presence of David Moriarty, Bishop of Kerry.

Walk 6

MOUNT EAGLE

6 miles (9.7 km) Moderate/Strenuous (see page 8)

```
0                              1 mile
|----+----+----+----+----|
0              1 km
```

This, the most westerly peak on the Dingle Peninsula, gives pleasant walking and the most stupendous views. To the north-east and east lie the other mountains of the peninsula: to the south is Dingle Bay and Valentia Island, while off the tip lies Great Blasket Island, like a monstrous whale. Beyond its outliers are thousands of miles of Atlantic Ocean.

1 *Take the R559 from Tralee through Dingle and Ventry, then take a left turn to the village of Kildurrihy and continue along this towards the TV mast. Park near here. Walk along the obvious green road which zigzags up to the saddle.*

2 *From here, continue along the green road to the cairned summit of Mount Eagle.*

3 *From the summit, bear to the right, then to the left (south-west) over Beenacouma, to follow the obvious shoulder over open hillside down to the road at Slea Head.*

4 *Turn left along the road towards Kilvickadown. Walk through the village, taking the right fork, then turning left at a T junction. Now follow the lane as it winds back to Kildurrihy, and your parked car.*

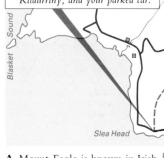

A Mount Eagle is known in Irish as Sliabh an Iolair. The summit is 1,695 feet (517 m) high. To the west lie the Blasket Islands – 'next parish America'. Great Blasket was permanently inhabited until 1953, and in the 19th century even the smaller islands had a few inhabitants. The nearest small island, Beiginis, had no permanent water, and was finally abandoned when the father of the only family living there was drowned while rowing across to Great Blasket for drinking water.

B The lower slopes of Mount Eagle, at Glenfahan, are strewn with relics of the distant past. A survey conducted about 60 years ago counted two promontory forts, 22 ring forts, 414 clocháns (dry stone beehive huts), 12 stone crosses, 19 pillar stones (two of these with ogham inscriptions), 19 souterrains (underground chambers of indeterminate use) and 29 other structures. Unfortunately many of these were cleared away before their worth was realised, but there is still much to see. The whole settlement covers several square miles, and it has been estimated that as many as 2000 people once lived in these townships, which have a history of occupation of one sort or another dating from prehistoric times until the 8 – 11th century.

THE PAPS

3.5 miles (5.6 km) Easy

0   1 mile
0   1 km

The Paps (or Da Chioch Dhana, the Two Breasts of [the Goddess] Dana) are so named for their distinctive outline when viewed from the west. They lie near the western boundary of Kerry. On a clear day, the summits provide grand views over great distances, coupled with a sense of being in a place where human associations stretch far back into the past.

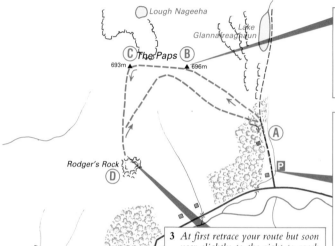

2 *Now walk to the summit of the western Pap, dropping at first, then ascending. From here, after enjoying the view, turn left (south) and walk for 0.5 mile (0.8 km) to arrive at the rocky outcrop known as Rodger's Rock.*

1 *From Killarney, drive for 10 miles (16 km) towards Cork on the N22, turning left over the Clydach River just after passing the school and church at Clonkeen. Follow this road for 2.5 miles (4 km), then turn left up a track which passes a small farm, parking your car near a small gravel pit. Walk up this track, which leads to Lake Glannafreaghaun (the Lake in the Valley of the Whortle-berry), until you come to a heather filled 'avenue' between pine trees on your left. Walk up this 'avenue', and from its top continue in the same direction over open ground to arrive at the summit of the eastern Pap at 2284 ft (696 m).*

3 *At first retrace your route but soon veer slightly to the right to reach the small saddle between the two Paps. Continuing in this direction, contour around the eastern Pap to arrive back at the top of the heather filled 'avenue' near the beginning of the walk. Descend this to join the track. Turn right and walk to your parked car.*

A This track follows the ancient southern approach route past Lake Glannafreaghaun (known locally as Shrone Lake), to Rathmore (An Rath Mhor, the Large Fort) and 'The City', a stone fort used in recent times as a Christian Penitential Station, but which dates from the Iron Age.

B From the summit, enjoy the panoramic view. 'The City' lies directly to the north. The large mound here and the one at the top of the western Pap are believed to

be prehistoric burial sites and are also associated with early pagan fertility rites. It was once thought that this area owed its prosperity to the Goddess Dana. The site of 'The City' is thought to be connected with the sisterhood of Dana, or Annul.

C The summit burial mound is in a very ruinous state, but what would appear to be an entrance way is clearly visible.

D This outcrop called Rodger's Rock was named after a herdsman employed by local farmers to mind their sheep and cattle in the high summer grazing areas. This transhumance farming method was commonly used in the recent past and was referred to locally as 'booleying'. From the rock, Rodger would summon aid by signalling other herdsmen by smoke or flag if anything went wrong.

Walk 8
CROHANE

4.5 miles (7.2 km) Moderate (see page 8)

Crohane Mountain towers over the south eastern side of Lough Guitane (Lake of the Garlands). The route to its summit, by track and open mountain, provides an ideal example of highland walking in Kerry. Throughout the course of the route and from the summit, extensive views of lakes, mountain landscape and rolling lowlands are to be enjoyed.

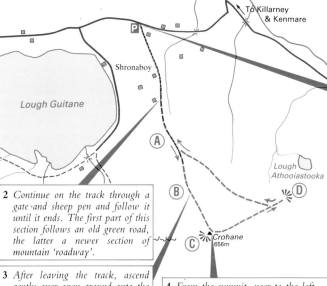

Lough Guitane

Shronaboy

Lough Athooiastooka

(A) (B) (C) (D)

Crohane 656m

1 *Take the N71 Kenmare Road from Killarney for 2.5 miles (4 km), then turn left on to the Lough Guitane road and follow this for a further 4 miles (6.4 km). The last 1.5 miles (2.4 km) skirts the northern edge of Lough Guitane, climbing up to Shronaboy where the lake eventually passes out of view. Park your car carefully on the roadside just before the road begins to descend.*
From the road follow the initially pine sheltered track on the right which leads up towards Crohane. The track passes a number of houses and continues behind farm buildings and up to Shronaboy proper – pause here to look over Lough Guitane, away to your right.

2 *Continue on the track through a gate and sheep pen and follow it until it ends. The first part of this section follows an old green road, the latter a newer section of mountain 'roadway'.*

3 *After leaving the track, ascend gently over open ground onto the wide northern shoulder of Crohane and head directly for the summit.*

4 *From the summit, veer to the left (north-east) and descend 200 ft (61 m) to a rocky outcrop where Lough Athooiastooka can be seen below. Now retrace your steps onto the* broad saddle you have just passed and, veering to the right, carefully descend to join the track used on your outward journey. Follow it downhill and return to your car.

A Having passed the sheep pen and joined the old green road, keep a look out for small ruined settlements and tillage plots, often known as lazy beds, dating from the pre-famine period (before 1845) of Irish history.

B Keep a look out for badger sets, red and sika deer and foxes.

C Having taken in the sweeping vistas, pay particular attention to the steep scree covered slopes of Bennaunmore, which stands immediately to your south-west. Bennaunmore is composed of hard volcanic rock. Its volcanic columns can be seen more clearly on the Cappagh Glen walk (no **10**).

D As you gaze down over Lough Athooiastooka, you will see the main Cork-Killarney road as it passes through Glenflesk. This valley was home of the O'Donoghues of the Glens, whose ruined castle can just be seen 2 miles (3.2 km) to the north. You can also see the now disused Crail Quarry; its stone was used as ballast for the old Killarney-Kenmare railway line which used to pass through the Glen on its way to Kilgarvan.

Walk 9
ESKDUFF, CAPPAGH AND STOOMPA

5 miles (8 km) Moderate (see page 8)

This fine walk takes you by three mountain lakes through quite remote terrain. It abounds with wildlife and provides bird's eye views into two spectacular glacial valleys.

Lough Guitane
Lough Nabrean (A)
Lough Garagarry
Eskduff Mountain
Cappagh Mountain
Cappagh River
(B)
(C)
Stoompa 693m
To Killarney & Kenmare
Owgarriff Bridge
Finow Bridge

1 Leave Killarney on the N71 towards Kenmare, turning left onto the Lough Guitane Road 2.5 miles (4 km) from the town. Follow this road for 3 miles (4.8 km). Turn right after passing over the small Owgarriff Bridge, then travel a further 0.5 mile (0.8 km) to where an unmetalled track on the right leads to a small pumping station on the Owgarriff River.

Park your car carefully near the entrance to this track.
Continue up this road on foot for 0.5 mile (0.8 km) before descending past a farmyard to Lough Guitane's south-west shore, where an old green road skirts the lake to the east. Follow this until the fourth stream cuts the route just south of Horse Island.

2 Follow this stream to Lough Nabrean, and walk around it with the water to your left until you reach another stream on the opposite side of the little lake.

3 Follow this stream up the hill, passing Eskduff on your left, and eventually arriving at the summit of Cappagh Mountain.

4 The higher summit ahead of you (to the west) is Stoompa at 2274 ft (693 m). Walk across open ground to this.

6 Follow the right hand bank of the stream, which forms the outlet to the lake, down to the pumping station. From here, follow the track which veers to the right (east), back to the starting point of the walk.

5 From the summit, descend down the spur to the right hand side (east) of Lough Garagarry (the Cormorants Lake) to join the lake on its far (northern) shore.

A Lough Nabrean provides a nesting ground for wild geese. Looking back down to Lough Guitane you will see, close in, Strawberry, Cow and Horse Islands. They were inhabited at one time as crannogs, or lake dwellings. Further out in the lake is Bare Island, which has a small harbour and a shooting butt (a shooter's stand behind a low wall).

B Look down onto Lough Guitane and into the Cappagh Glen (see Walk **10**), but take care, the drop below you into the oak wooded glen is nearly 1,000 ft (305 m). Notice the scree covered slopes across the valley buttress, and the volcanic plug of Bennaunmore.

C The spectacular glacial valley below is the Horses Glen with its three lakes – Enhagh, Monagh and Gaeigre. **Do not be tempted to go down to them.**

Walk 10
CAPPAGH GLEN
5 miles (8 km) Moderate – but can be slippery

The Cappagh Glen walk circuits the volcanic rocks of the scree sloped Bennaunmore, passing through a landscape shaped by glacial ice and the spate-streams which flow into beautiful Loch Guitane. The walk provides a great contrast of mountain scenery ranging from open views to the deep and narrow rock walled Cappagh Glen, which protects the two small native oak woods from which the glen derives its name ('Ceapach' meaning decayed or denuded wood in Gaelic).

A Look back over Lough Guitane, which now serves as a reservoir supplying the town of Tralee, some 24 miles (38.6 km) away. The stone building at the outlet from the lake is the pump-house. Keep a look out for deer as they bound over the slopes of Crohane Mountain (see Walk **8**).

B The remains of the pathway and the stone uprights you now see are probably part of an old drove or pilgrims road, a branch of which still skirts the northern shoulder of Crohane. This road is probably the northern end of the long pilgrimage route from the plains of North Kerry through Kilgarvan or the Roughty Valley to Gougane Barra. If you should follow Walk **25**, you will meet the other end of this pilgrims' way, where it descends into Gougane Barra, a pilgrimage centre of great renown. Pilgrims from all over Cork and Kerry used to gather for the festival of St Finbar on Gougane Sunday at the end of September. Finbar built a small monastery at Gougane before moving to Cork, where his name is remembered there in St Finbar's Cathedral.

C On the far (west) side of Lough Nabroda are the cliffs on Bennaunmore. They have been compared with the Giant's Causeway, but really the only point of similarity is that they are formed of polygonal columns. Bennaunmore was probably part of the crater of a volcano from the Devonian Period, nearly the same age as the surrounding Old Red Sandstone. The rock is rhyolite, an acid rock at the other end of the scale from the basic basalt of the Giant's Causeway. The columns, which are about 200 ft (60 m) high, were formed by the rapid cooling of the molten rock into this shape. The name Bennaunmore comes from the Irish Beann Mhór, big peak. This may seem a rather honorific title for a summit which is only 1490 ft (454 m) in height, but it must be admitted that end on it is an impressive sight.

D J C Coleman, an ardent and knowledgeable walker in both Cork and Kerry, and the first person to write a walkers' guide to the Kerry Mountains, reported (in 1948) that on a well-preserved portion of the old trail where it winds under a big crag, there is 'an ice-smoothed rock . . . having names and initials carved on it'. These, it is assumed, are the names of pilgrims who passed on their way to Gougane Sunday, but succeeding guide writers have all failed to find this rock.

E Looking south and south-east gives fine views of Morley's Bridge and into the valley of the River Raughty – at the end of which is the highest pub in Ireland.

F This woodland is of native oak and is one of the few remaining in the Killarney area. 'Ceapach' can mean decayed or denuded wood, and it is from this that this small river valley derives its name. Many of the oak-woods of Iveragh and Beara were cut down in the late 17th century to make charcoal for iron smelting furnaces. Perhaps the remoteness and difficulty of access of this glen saved the trees. Sadly, many of those at the southern end are leafless, and have been dubbed 'the petrified forest'. On the walk through the valley you may spot falcons, which occasionally rest on the cliffs above you. The observant will also spot marbled surfaces on a few of the boulders they pass, further evidence of the volcanic history of the rocks of this area.

Over

1 Take the N71 road from Killarney to Kenmare for 2.5 miles (4 km) before turning left onto the Lough Guitane road. Follow this road for 4 miles (6.4 km) and turn right taking the road which skirts the eastern side of the Lake. Park your car before the bridge which crosses the Cappagh River, making sure not to obstruct the bridge which leads into a farmyard.

The road leading to the bridge is joined by a track. Follow this track as far as a disused house (now used as a farm shed) and, from here, follow the stream which descends from the outcrop to the west of Crohane.

2 Ignoring the first tributary on the left, which comes down from Crohane, climb up to 1200 ft (366 m) using what remains of the old pathway to Kilgarvan. Bearing to the right, you come onto a boggy plateau where stone uprights may have served to mark out this section of the old route.

3 Having enjoyed the view, you now turn left (south) to walk towards Lough Nabrada. Walk along its left hand (eastern) shore. This lake is fed by a stream from a second lake higher up the narrow valley. Climbing up the valley, over a boggy section of ground, will bring you to Crohane Lake, which should be skirted on its right hand (western) side until a wooded area is reached. From here turn right directly up the slope to arrive over the steep-sided head of the Cappagh Glen.

5 Follow this stream down the valley, at first on its left hand (western) side, but quickly changing to its right hand (eastern) bank. The valley now narrows with the masses of Bennaunmore and Eskduff Mountains towering above. Where the valley broadens, a second stand of oak can be seen. The path passes this before climbing a small boulder field onto a saddle on the western flank of Bennaunmore. The route now drops gently to arrive at the beginning of a track which skirts the mountain and leads through shallow fords to pass the old farm building and the bridge at the start of the walk.

4 Now veer right (north) over open ground until you reach the saddle before the peak of Bennaunmore. From here descend carefully down into the Cappagh Valley. **This section of the walk should be undertaken with extreme care, particularly in wet or misty weather, due to the many mossy, slippery boulders.** You will arrive on the edge of a small native oak wood, along which flows a small stream.

MANGERTON MOUNTAIN
6 miles (9.7 km) Moderate (see page 8)

This is a relatively easy walk to the top of a high mountain, one of the few in Ireland which actually has a track for most of the way. It takes you easily amongst magnificent rocky cirques (bowl-shaped valleys) to a summit, and is an excellent first walk for anyone planning to explore the Killarney area. Choose a fine, clear day to enjoy the extensive views over lakes, hills and sea.

1 Take the Kenmare road (N71) out of Killarney, turn off left just beyond the Muckross Hotel onto the road signposted 'Mangerton Viewing Park'. Turn sharp right where the road leaves the wood and drive along a narrow road beside the wood to the bridge over the Finoulagh River. Park by the bridge.
Follow the track, at first beside the river, and then up the heathery hillside. The track bears right around the mountain shoulder and follows an old boundary fence to the outlet of the lake in the Devil's Punchbowl.

5 Now walk back to your car, following your original route.

4 Return to the escarpment overlooking the Devil's Punchbowl, and walk with the lake to your right, descending the ridge to rejoin your outward route at the Punchbowl outlet.

2 The track fades out. Walk over stony ground along the left hand (north) side of the lake and then climb up quite steeply to the ridge between the Devil's Punchbowl and Glenacappul.

3 Follow the ridge to the summit plateau, and then walk to the small summit cairn ahead at 2746 ft (837 m).

A This is the pony track used by 19th-century tourists.

B Tooreencormick is the site of a battle in 1262 in which the MacCarthy Mor clan defeated an Anglo-Norman army under Gerald de Roche. De Roche and Cormick MacCarthy (after whom the battle was named) were both killed.

C This is the small dam for Killarney's water supply. The beehive hut is not ancient. It was built for gamekeepers just a century ago.

D The Devil's Punchbowl lake is reputed to be bottomless. There is a story about a certain Charles Fox who dived in and was never seen again – but who later wrote from Australia asking for his clothes.

E Pause to get your breath, and look down to your right at the Devil's Punchbowl, and to the left down into Glenacappul (The Horse's Glen).

F Mangerton may mean 'the hairy one', refering to the long grass on its plateau. It is a magnificent viewpoint over the Killarney Lakes to the north-west; the Ridge of the Reeks marching away to the west; to Corrán Tuathail Mountain, at 3409 ft (1039 m) the highest mountain in Ireland (see Walk **17**), and the long Kenmare River (actually a fjord) to the south-west.

MUCKROSS PARK AND DINIS ISLAND

7 miles (11.3 km) Easy

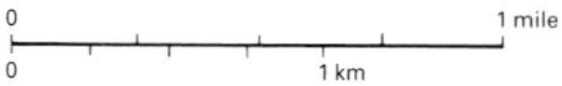

A fine, easy walk around a lake which nestles in the shadow of the towering MacGillycuddy's Reeks.

You can include visits to Muckross Abbey and Muckross House, so allow a whole day for this walk, if you can, and bring a picnic. This walk can be linked with Walk **13**.

1 *Take the main N71 road, to Kenmare from Killarney, to the Muckross Hotel. Leave your car in the car park on the right hand side. Follow the sign to nearby Muckross Abbey.*

2 *Having explored the Abbey, continue along the path, following the signpost on your left to Dinis. Soon the main avenue of Muckross House comes into view.*

3 *Take a right turn past an estate house. Continue along this pathway to Brickeen Bridge and Dinis Island.*

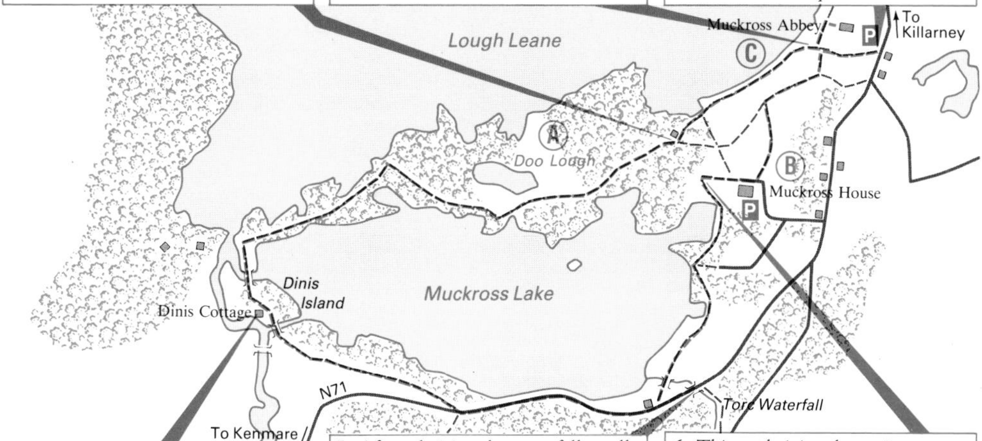

4 *At Dinis Cottage, turn left along a path leading to the main Kenmare Road. Turn left to walk to the bridge below the Torc Waterfall.*

5 *After admiring the waterfall, walk back a little way along the road and turn right onto a path which runs beside Muckross Lake, and leads towards Muckross House.*

6 *This path joins the main avenue. Visit Muckross House, or follow this path through some pleasant parklands back to the Abbey, and your car.*

A A thriving herd of Kerry cattle can usually be seen here, grazing within the National Park. This breed originated in Asia, and was brought here late in the Stone Age. For centuries it was the staple of the economic and monetary system in Ireland, and is ideally suited to the uplands of Kerry and Cork. This particular pure bred herd is owned and supported by the state.

B Muckross House was built in 1843 in neo-Tudor style by the Herbert family. In 1861 Queen Victoria and her hundred strong party were entertained here in lavish style. Today the house is a National Folk Museum, with a variety of craftsmen resident. An excellent leaflet, giving details of the National Park, is available here.

C Muckross Abbey was founded in 1448 by the local Chief McCarthy-More for the Franciscan Friars. It was built on the site of a church destroyed by fire in the 12th century. Long unaffected by the reformation, it suffered its share of trauma later on. In 1589 a party of English soldiers raided the abbey and tortured to death two of the Friars, although another escaped with the treasures of the abbey to hide on the nearby islands.

Walk 13
TORC MOUNTAIN
5 miles (8 km) Moderate – but no dogs (see page 8)

Torc Mountain, named after the wild boar that once roamed its slopes, lies in the heart of the Killarney National Park. Although a relatively small hill, the summit offers superb views of the surrounding countryside. Its steep rhododendron-covered north face towers over Muckross Lake and gives a great sense of loftiness. The area to the south of Torc is a favourite haunt of red deer. This walk can be linked with Walk **12**.

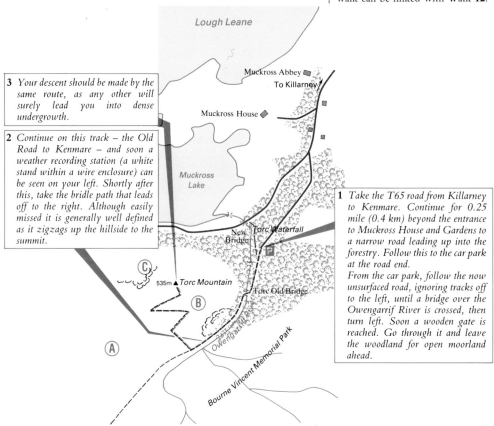

3 *Your descent should be made by the same route, as any other will surely lead you into dense undergrowth.*

2 *Continue on this track – the Old Road to Kenmare – and soon a weather recording station (a white stand within a wire enclosure) can be seen on your left. Shortly after this, take the bridle path that leads off to the right. Although easily missed it is generally well defined as it zigzags up the hillside to the summit.*

1 *Take the T65 road from Killarney to Kenmare. Continue for 0.25 mile (0.4 km) beyond the entrance to Muckross House and Gardens to a narrow road leading up into the forestry. Follow this to the car park at the road end.*
From the car park, follow the now unsurfaced road, ignoring tracks off to the left, until a bridge over the Owengarrif River is crossed, then turn left. Soon a wooden gate is reached. Go through it and leave the woodland for open moorland ahead.

Map labels: Lough Leane; Muckross Abbey; To Killarney; Muckross House; Muckross Lake; New Bridge; Torc Waterfall; Torc Old Bridge; 535m Torc Mountain; Owengarrif; Bourne Vincent Memorial Park; A; B; C

A On your ascent take time to view the moorland behind you. It is particularly rich in wildlife so look out for red deer, mountain hares, badgers and foxes, as well as kestrels and sparrow-hawks.

B The signs of past habitation are many, with numerous ruined settlements and tillage plots. This area was lived in up to the Clearances (1845-50) – when the landowners evicted people in order to hunt more effectively.

C From the summit of Torc, look out for peregrine falcons over the north-west side.

PURPLE AND TOMIES MOUNTAINS

8 miles (12.9 km) Strenuous (see page 8)

This is an unmarked but safe route onto the high mountains. Both peaks visited give superb views of the MacGillycuddy's Reeks, Dingle Bay, the plains of Mid Kerry, Killarney, and the Black Valley. The walk starts at Kate Kearney's Cottage, a popular pub and restaurant which takes its name from a local 19th-century beauty. This route can be linked with Walk **16**.

1 *From Killarney take the R562 westwards to Beaufort. Turn right in the village and follow the signposts for the Gap of Dunloe. Park at Kate Kearneys Cottage. Walk up the road through the Gap, passing three lakes, until you reach its highest point. From here, turn left (east) to leave the road and follow the course of a broken down fence. Soon you will meet a stream and walled fence running down towards you. Veer left (north-east) and follow this upstream to Glas Lough.*

5 *Follow the track leading out from the field to the main road. Turn left at the road to walk just less than 0.5 mile (0.8 km) back to Kate Kearneys Cottage.*

4 *Now veer slightly left, descending the stony northern slopes to a boggy col. Continue in this direction (north-west) over open ground, keeping Tomies Rock well to your left, and then veer to the right along the spur running down towards the large green field below.*

3 *Maintain your direction, following sheep tracks, along the ridge towards Tomies Mountain. At the next summit bear left (north), crossing the boggy saddle leading to the summit of Tomies Mountain.*

2 *Walk along the left hand side of the lake. At the end of the lake follow another fence, which runs to the right, uphill to its end. From here, bear left up the stony slope to the summit of Purple Mountain, which is marked by a cairn.*

A As you head into the Gap of Dunloe, pause here for a rest before tackling the hill above. The larger ruined building on the left side of the road served for many years, until 1921, as a barracks for the Royal Irish Constabulary. It was garrisoned by 21 men whose job it was to protect the pass for the lucrative tourist industry pioneered by Thomas Cook & Co of London. On the right are the ruins of Arbutus Cottage, where superb engraved furniture was once made.

B The Gap of Dunloe has been used as a pass for centuries, although it was not until the 19th century that the local Landlord – O'Mahoney of Dunloe Castle, built a rough road through it.

Walk 15
OLD KENMARE ROAD
7 miles (11.3 km) one way. Easy – but no dogs

This walk follows the Old Kenmare Road, which was the main route between Killarney and Kenmare before being closed during 'The Clearances' (1845-50) by landowners who wanted to reserve the land for deer hunting rather than farming. The walk reveals unusual views of the Killarney area and provides a great opportunity to see both red deer and Japanese sika deer. The full route requires two cars, or a chauffeur willing to deposit and collect those walking, since there is no public transport available here. But since this is such a fine walk, it is well worth the trouble of arranging transport, or just walking part of the way, having a picnic and returning by the same route.

The whole of this walk follows the waymarks of The Kerry Way; these are in the form of yellow arrows on dark timber or plastic posts, with an occasional yellow 'walking man' symbol.

2 *Continuing in a northerly direction, the track now descends through the Windy Gap towards the Eagles' Nest (not to be confused with the better known Eagles' Nest north of the Upper Lake). Follow the path towards Galway's Bridge. Use the large stepping stones to carefully ford the stream.*

1 *From the small park in the centre of Kenmare take the road signposted for the hospital. After 0.5 mile (0.8 km) take the right fork in the road and follow this for a further 2 miles (3.2 km) uphill until the T junction at Gowlane is reached. Park here. The track ahead is the beginning of the walk. Follow the track as it climbs gently up to the col between Peakean Mountain and Knockanaguish.*

A Look to the south and west for sweeping views over Kenmare and Kenmare River to the peninsula.

B Watch out for signs of old habitation all along the walk; sections of old roadways, tillage beds, ruined houses, walled gardens and orchards.

C You now enter the Killarney National Park. Unlike most Parks in Britain or Continental Europe, the State owns all the property within the Park boundaries. While this clearly limits the area which can become a Park, it does mean that any development can be very closely controlled.

D On the slopes on either side roam the only herd of native red deer remaining in Ireland. Now numbering over 400 animals, the herd is believed to have existed continuously since the arrival of red deer in Ireland after the last Ice Age. There are also very many Japanese sika deer, introduced by landowners in the last century. While the red deer do seem to be increasing in numbers, they are carefully protected, and this is definitely not a place for dogs. The strange structure up on your right is used for deer spotting by the Park Rangers.

E The Torc Waterfall is perhaps the finest in the Killarney area, and well worth a visit.

Over

Map labels:
Continued 2 miles
Windy Gap
Cummeenslaun Lake
Peakeen Mountain 555m
Knockanaguish 509m
A
Gowlane
P
To Kenmare

0   1 mile

0   1 km

5 *On entering Esknamucky Glen the route follows the course of the stream, passing through a small steeply sided and wooded section of the valley. When the valley broadens, cross the small stream and walk to the waterfall known as Cores Cascade. The stream flowing from the cascade must be crossed. This should be done a little downstream.*

4 *The Old Kenmare Road is not well defined along this section of the walk, but you can easily maintain your direction (north-east) by heading towards towards Esknamucky Glen and following the waymarks. Small sections of the old road soon reappear, and are easily followed.*

7 *The track now passes through a gate and enters woodland as it begins to descend. The stream the path now follows eventually thunders over the famous Torc Waterfall. Pass a one bar gate and turn right over the wooden bridge – the old stone one is now in ruins. Continue on to the car park.*

Muckross Lake

Torc Waterfall

E

P

▲
Torc Mountain

D

6 miles

C

6 *Having crossed the stream maintain your direction until the track is picked up as it leaves the glen, climbing up between the mountains of Mangerton (see Walk 11) and Torc (see Walk 13). Follow the track over open ground for 2 miles (3.2 km).*

4 miles

Esknamucky Glen

Cores Cascade

Galway's Bridge

B

Shaking Rock

3 *After crossing the stream pass a small farmstead on your left and join the tarred road for a short distance, turning off to your right where the path begins again. This is marked with a signpost.*

Eagle's Nest

Signpost

Continued

31

Walk 16
CNOC AN BHRACA and the GAP OF DUNLOE
12 miles (19.3 km) Moderate

After Killarney itself, the Gap of Dunloe is probably the biggest tourist attraction in Kerry. This can sometimes be unfortunate for the walker who prefers solitude, because the scenery is so magnificent that it should not be missed. So be prepared to see other visitors, but do try to avoid holiday weekends, if you can. This walk takes you easily over the summits to the west of the Gap, and brings you back down the Gap itself. Once you have overcome the steep zigzag path out of the valley the going is fairly easy. Please remember however that once you are on the top of the hills, there are high cliffs between you and the valley, and you must either continue until you can descend at the south end of the Gap, or retrace your footsteps; *there are no short cuts*. If you want a longer walk, follow this route to the south end of the Gap, and return by Walk **14** over Purple Mountain.

A Kate Kearneys Cottage is a famous pub and restaurant, and the starting point for all those who wish to ponytrek through the Gap.

B This track was built in the last century as a bog road for the removal of peat from the highland bogs above.

C Cnoc an Bhraca is the first peak on the classic Reek Ridge traverse, which begins in the Gap and follows the magnificent ridge line over all the Reeks to the end at the western extremity near Glencar. Views stretch into Ireland's premier mountain valley off to the west, the Hags Glen surrounded by the MacGillycuddy's Reeks, and Corrán Tuathail itself (see Walk **17**), standing impressively at the head of the valley.

Until a few years ago, there used to be an organised 'Reeks Walk', traversing the length of the Reeks Ridge, with several hundred participants, on the first Saturday in June. The organisers stopped it because the massed tread of so many people was severely damaging the delicate vegetation cover on the ridge, and creating serious erosion. These craggy hills look as though they could stand up to any number of boots, but the heather and bog sections are very fragile, and once the cover is damaged, the shortness of the growing season prevents re-growth.

The next peak to the west, Cruach Mhór (the big stack), 3162 ft (964 m), is notable for a small grotto at its summit. This was built with great labour by an old man who lived in the valley to the north. He carried all the materials up himself, even bringing water to mix concrete from Lough Cummeenapeasta (the lake of the hollow of the serpent) 1000 ft (305 m) below.

D This col was part of the old funeral route from the southern parts of the parish to Tough – The Black Valley – and beyond to the cemetery down by the River Laune. Pall bearers carried the coffin over this col around Cnoc an Bhraca on its east side and down to the townlands west of Strickeen. There are views along the southern slopes of the Reeks and into the Black Valley to the south.

E As you walk along the Gap road, the dramatic cliffs of Purple and Bull mountains tower above you. These are home to breeding pairs of Peregrine Falcons, which can often be seen soaring overhead.

F Down by the Auger Lake, two old ruins can be seen on the roadside. The larger of these was, until 1921, a barracks for the Royal Irish Constabulary. At the turn of this century, some 21 men were garrisoned here to protect the pass for the lucrative tourist industry pioneered by Thomas Cook & Co of London. The other ruin is that of Arbutus Cottage, where superb engraved furniture was once made.

G During the Ice Age, the Kerry Mountains had their own glaciers. The Gap of Dunloe was formed by one such glacier which overflowed over the ridge, and then cut its way down to form the deep narrow valley. It has always been a crucial pass for travellers and although a track of sorts has existed for centuries, the foundations of the present road were laid during the mid 1800s.

Over

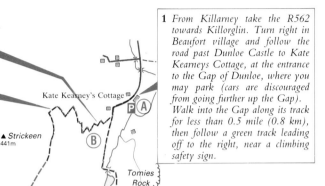

2 *Follow this green track as it gently zigzags up along the hillside.*

3 *The track ascends to a 'scare-crow' tree before swinging left (south) into open bogland. The 1446 ft (441 m) summit of Strickeen, with its two cairns, is off to your right.*

4 *Maintain your direction towards the peak of Cnoc an Bhraca, 'the Rough Hill'. Firm strong ground for some 700 feet (213 m) helps you attain its summit.*

5 *From here, veer left (south-east) onto a grassy col, losing 500 ft (152 m) to make the short rise up again to the large boulders that mark the top of the Bull Mountain.*

6 *From the Bull, follow the obvious ridge line (running south) to Drishana and further still to the road beyond. Note that it is **very dangerous** to attempt to descend earlier on this section to the beckoning Gap road below. Steep craggy ground obstructs the way.*

1 *From Killarney take the R562 towards Killorglin. Turn right in Beaufort village and follow the road past Dunloe Castle to Kate Kearneys Cottage, at the entrance to the Gap of Dunloe, where you may park (cars are discouraged from going further up the Gap). Walk into the Gap along its track for less than 0.5 mile (0.8 km), then follow a green track leading off to the right, near a climbing safety sign.*

7 *Once on the road, and having savoured the views down to Killarney's upper lake, turn left and return over the head of the Gap. Some 5 miles (8 km) of track through the pass will lead you back to the starting point.*

33

Walk 17
CORRÁN TUATHAIL MOUNTAIN
8 miles (12.9 km) Strenuous (see page 8) – unsuitable when the Gaddagh River is in spate

Corrán Tuathail is Ireland's highest peak at 3409 ft (1039 m) and, as such, is quite challenging to reasonably experienced hill-walkers. Save this walk for a fine, clear day so that you can enjoy the stunning views to the full. The route described is the regular tourist route via the Hag's Glen and the Devil's Ladder, where a rough track exists for most of the way to the summit. This track is always stony and often loose, and, occasionally, the cairns can be quite confusing (especially in mist) due to the amount of natural stone around.

From the start of the walk some 800 ft (244 m) are gained pleasantly over 2 miles (3.2 km) before the Hag's Glen is entered. This glen, with its many glaciated side coombs, is an awe inspiring spot, enclosed by the MacGillycuddy's Reeks all around. The Ladder is a loose scree gully of some 600 ft (188 m) in height and gives access to a grassy col above. From here a cairned track leads 0.75 mile (1.2 km) up the final 1000 ft (305 m) to the top.

A The Gaddagh River's high eroded banks are the result of an incredible flash flood in 1916, which took with it practically all the bridges in the Beaufort area at that time.

B Farming of some sort has always gone on in this glen – after crossing the Gaddagh River down near Cronin's Farm, green areas cleared of stones can be seen; these were once small tillage plots.

C The Hags Glen (Coomb Callee) is named after an unkempt woman who once lived here towards the latter part of the 18th century.

D In Gaelic Corrán is a sickle or serrated peak, whilst Tuathail may be derived from the name of a tribe.

E The MacGillycuddy's Reeks – originally Na Cruacha Dubha, the black stacks, are named after a local family of landlords who were resident in the west of Beaufort on the banks of the Laune River.

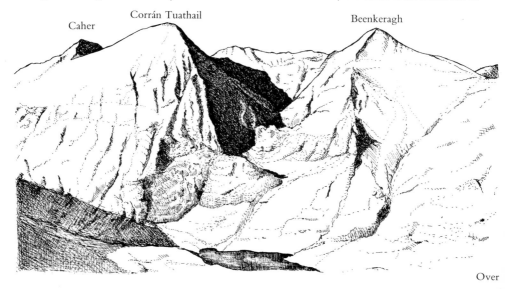

Caher   Corrán Tuathail   Beenkeragh

Over

34

0   1 mile

0   1 km

1 *From Killarney take the main Killorgin Road, and, after 5 miles (8 km) turn left at the Beaufort Bridge. Follow the signs to the Corrán Tuathail Youth Hostel. Continue past the youth hostel to Cronin's farmyard, at the road end. Cars may be parked in the farmyard for a small fee.* **The Cronin's advice should be sought if there is any doubt about conditions on the hill.**
Follow the track leading from the farmyard, which is quite muddy at first, until the Black Stream is crossed. Just beyond this stream the track forks – take the right fork. A little further on the main Gaddagh River has to be crossed, using the stones. **Do not attempt this when the river is in spate.**

4 *From here follow the cairned route to the top. The summit is clearly marked by a large steel cross and cairn.*

5 *Return by the same route, taking care not to lose your track.*

2 *After the river, follow the track up the hillside. Soon it intersects with a more established stony road. Follow this road into the Glen. About 1 mile (1.6 km) further on, the river is re-crossed over stepping stones. The track continues and soon Lough Callee, with its island Oileán an Callee (the Hag's Island), comes into view, followed by Lough Gouragh, (the Goats Lake), on the right. The track continues, slightly less defined but adequately clear, to rise up towards the foot of the Devil's Ladder, the obvious scree scar running down from the col, to the left of Corrán Tuathail.*

3 *The Ladder is extremely loose and the route by the right-hand wall of the gully is recommended. Keep close together if in a group so as to avoid any danger from loose stones, and beware of people above you. The top of the gully is composed of quite slippery clay, but leads to the pleasant col.*

To Killarney

Gaddagh River

▲ Cloghfaunaglibbaun

Youth Hostel

Knocknafreaghaun

Knockroe

P

Black Stream

A

B

▲ Knockbrinnea
830m

▲ Beenkeragh
1010m

D

Lough Gouragh

C

Lough Callee

Corrán Tuathail
▲ 1039m

Hag's Glen

The Devil's Ladder

▲

Curraghmore Lake

THE MACGILLYCUDDY'S REEKS

E

MOUNTAIN STAGE TO KELLS

6 miles (9.7 km) one way. Easy   **VIA THE OLD COACH ROAD**

0 _____ 1 mile
0 _____ 1 km

The route follows The Old Coach Road, which was built in the late 18th century, and rises to 1200 ft (366 m) as it skirts the slopes between Drung Hill and Dingle Bay. Still known as the 'Butter Road', it was used to carry firkins of butter to the Cork Butter Exchange. As you follow the road, imagine the anxiety of those who passed this way in swaying horse drawn coaches. Indeed Daniel O'Connell, the first Irish catholic to sit in the House of Commons, was pitched from his carriage when his horse fell along here. Lower down is the tunnelled and viaducted railway line built in the late 1800's but now unfortunately disused. Along the Old Coach Road you will see the waymarks of 'The Kerry Way' – a walking man.

A one way walk along this route requires two cars, or a chauffeur willing to deposit and collect those walking, since there is no public transport available here. If this is impossible to arrange, an 'out and back' walk along part, or all, of the route from either end, will not disappoint. The walk as described finishes at the bay at Kells.

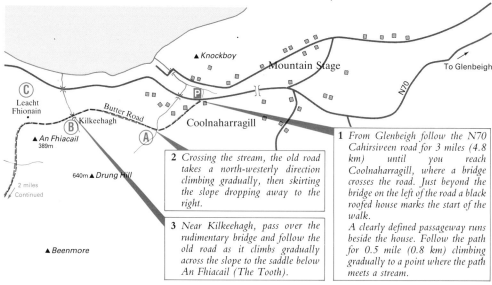

2 *Crossing the stream, the old road takes a north-westerly direction climbing gradually, then skirting the slope dropping away to the right.*

3 *Near Kilkeehagh, pass over the rudimentary bridge and follow the old road as it climbs gradually across the slope to the saddle below An Fhiacail (The Tooth).*

1 *From Glenbeigh follow the N70 Cahirsiveen road for 3 miles (4.8 km) until you reach Coolnaharragill, where a bridge crosses the road. Just beyond the bridge on the left of the road a black roofed house marks the start of the walk.*
A clearly defined passageway runs beside the house. Follow the path for 0.5 mile (0.8 km) climbing gradually to a point where the path meets a stream.

A In early summer the insectivorous common butterwort may be seen in wet places. This graceful perennial, with its violet and white flower and basal rosette of pale green leaves, was once believed to cause fatal disease in sheep. The larger greater butterwort or bog violet may also be seen. Both flower in May and June.

B Though no obvious signs remain today, Bothan na nUbh (the Hut of the Eggs) stood hereabouts. This house, well known to travellers in the 1700's and 1800's, housed an old woman who sold eggs to passers-by, although it is hinted that the hut was a 'shebeen' (a drinking den) which also provided a drop of spiritual support.

C On approaching the saddle a standing stone (gallaun) called Leacht Fhionain (the monument of St Fionan) appears. This, like many other such stones, was re-dedicated in spite of its pre-Christian origins, and now bears a cross and Ogham inscriptions (Ogham is a 6th century Celtic script – see page 11). To your right (north) there are fine views over

Over

0   1 mile
0   1 km

Dingle Bay and half-left ahead (south-west) a superb view of the bay of the Valentia River at Cahirsiveen.

D Gleensk Viaduct can be seen to the north-west. It carried the railway line, which opened in 1893 and closed in 1960, to Cahirsiveen and Valentia Harbour.

E The route so far has followed the Coach or 'Butter' Road. The builders of these roads preferred where possible to build in straight lines and a quick glance at a map will confirm this. You can see the old road following a straight path through Linateerha, Foilmore, Moneyduff and into Cahirsiveen.

The Old Coach Road

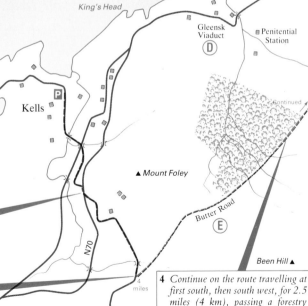

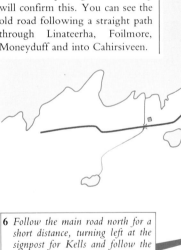

King's Head

Feaklecally

Gleensk Viaduct

D

Penitential Station

Kells

Mount Foley

Butter Road

E

Been Hill ▲

N70

Continued

6 Follow the main road north for a short distance, turning left at the signpost for Kells and follow the road down to the village and the pretty little bay. Meet your car here, or have a picnic and a rest if you are walking back.

5 At the junction of the minor road, turn right (north), leaving The Kerry Way, and enjoy an easy walk down to the main Glenbeigh to Cahirsiveen road (N70).

4 miles

4 Continue on the route travelling at first south, then south west, for 2.5 miles (4 km), passing a forestry plantation about half way. The old road now meets a minor road.

ROSSBEIGH HILL

4 miles (6.4 km) Easy

Viewed from Glenbeigh, Rossbeigh Hill looks like a giant tonsured head, this appearance being created by the thick forestry which grows along the base and lower slopes, with the crown of the hill left bare. This is an easy walk with superb views over Dingle Bay and Rossbeigh Strand, and an opportunity to look down onto Winn's Folly.

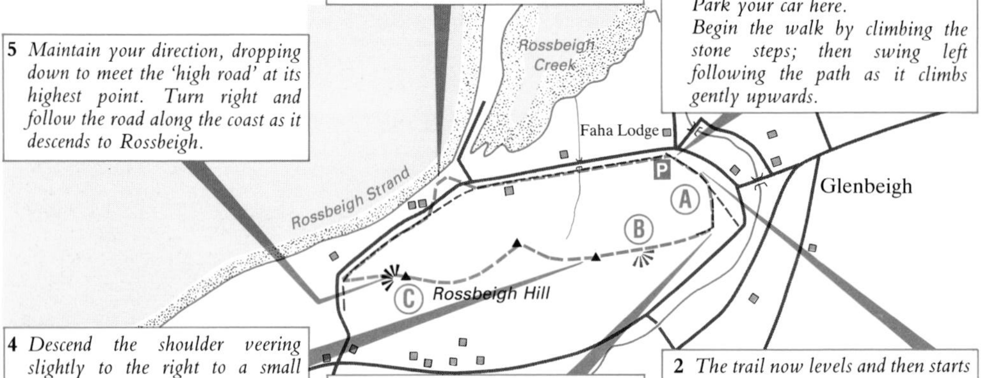

1 *From the village of Glenbeigh, head towards Rossbeigh Strand, which is clearly signposted. Follow the road over a small bridge, turning right and continuing for a short distance until a picnic site is seen on the left at Faha Lodge. Park your car here.*
Begin the walk by climbing the stone steps; then swing left following the path as it climbs gently upwards.

6 *A small detour onto the strand is worth the effort. Follow the road back towards Glenbeigh and Faha Lodge, where you began the walk.*

5 *Maintain your direction, dropping down to meet the 'high road' at its highest point. Turn right and follow the road along the coast as it descends to Rossbeigh.*

4 *Descend the shoulder veering slightly to the right to a small saddle, then continue to the true summit of Rossbeigh Hill. From here swing to the left to drop to another saddle, and then veer right to ascend to the last summit, which is marked by a stone cairn.*

3 *Turn right here and climb uphill to cross a stone wall. Follow what remains of the wall up to the first summit of the hill.*

2 *The trail now levels and then starts to descend slightly. A narrower path meets the track from the left and continues up on the right. Follow this path, which becomes a little stony, until it is crossed by yet another path.*

Rossbeigh Creek

Faha Lodge

Rossbeigh Strand

Glenbeigh

Rossbeigh Hill

A This section of the walk is particularly attractive in autumn when the mixture of trees provides a beautiful display of colours, accentuating the lovely views over Rossbeigh Strand and Glenbeigh.

B Look back to the east, to the startling Glenbeigh Towers (or Winn's Folly). The building was commissioned by the fourth Lord Headley of Aghadoe in 1867. Lord Headley took action against its architect W.E. Godwin because costs had exceeded the estimate and the walls and roofs leaked. The affair was finally settled in 1875. The Winns were again in the centre of disputes in the late 1880's when 70 of their tenants were brutally evicted by Lord Headley. These 'Glenbeigh Evictions' were hotly debated in the House of Commons and given much publicity by *The Times* newspaper. The Towers were gutted by fire in 1922.

C As you travel west, there are sweeping views over Dingle Bay as far as the Blasket Islands, which stand in the Atlantic off Slea Head. This is an area well known for the Gaelic language and its rich literature.

KNOCKNADOBAR BY THE PILGRIM'S ROUTE

6.5 miles (10.5 km) Moderate

This walk follows the Pilgrims route, along which the 14 Stations of the Cross were erected in 1885 by Canon Brosnan, to the summit of Knocknadobar. As the ascent steepens the route zigzags, allowing time to gain breath and contemplate the High Cross above. 'Cnoc na dTobar' is the mountain's Gaelic name – it means the Hill of the Wells. There are sweeping views over Dingle Bay to Slea Head and the Dingle Peninsula from the top.

2 *When you reach the cross continue in the same direction, over eroded turf, to the true summit, which is marked by a small cairn, at 2267 ft (691 m).*

3 *Now veer right (east) to the shoulder and down a sharp ridge over the Glendalough Lakes.* **Take care on this section, since it follows a short strech of narrow ridge.** *Continue down over open ground onto a broad saddle.*

4 *A path can be seen on the saddle. Go down to this, and walk to the right (south-west) along it until it meets the line of an old road. Follow this down to the Holy Well from where you started. (The line of this road is not always discernible, being somewhat overgrown, but its direction is clearly visible due to the ruins of stone buildings which line its route.)*

A sign states 'Stations Next Gate'. Pass through the gate and ascend following the clearly visible route.

1 *Take the Glenbeigh road from Cahirsiveen for 2 miles (3.2 km), then turn left for Coonanna Harbour. After 1.5 miles (2.4 km) you will find a small grotto to the right: park your car here.*

A The Stations, painted white, were built in thanksgiving by the local parish priest when the roof of his church in nearby Foilmore survived a fierce winter storm. It isn't known whether the tradition of pilgrimage here dates from before 1885.

B Look out for the greater butterwort (also known as bog violet), which is considered by many to be the most beautiful of Irish flora; it is rich violet in colour. This plant does not grow in Britain, being confined to the south west of Ireland. It also occurs in the Jura mountains, the French Alps and the Pyrenees.

C The High Cross, known as the Canon's Cross, does not mark the true summit. Mass is celebrated here on the annual pilgrimage.

D The path here is called 'Cnoc na mBo' (the Hill of the Cows) and was used for herding cattle from Kells to Cahirsiveen Fair.

E The Holy Well at the back of the neatly hedged house before the grotto is dedicated to St. Fursey and is believed to offer cures for eye complaints.

MULLAGHANATTIN

5 miles (8 km) Strenuous (see page 8)

Mullaghanattin is a fine mountain and, standing a little apart, makes an excellent viewpoint for the MacGillycuddy's Reeks. There are also grand views over the wild and tangled mountains to the west. This walk is quite short, but both the ascent and descent are steep. Although this route is straight-forward in good visibility, and recommended as an easily-acquired Kerry 'top', **it should not be undertaken in mist** as there are crags on both sides of the ridge.

3 From here walk directly up open ground to the summit. It is a steep but straightforward ascent.

2 To the right of the coomb, a stone wall heading almost directly for the summit, leads you part way up the mountain, to a large ledge, near the site of Temple Dermot.

1 Take the Killarney to Sneem road (first N71, then R568) and turn right (north-west) onto the road to the Ballaghbeama Pass. Immediately after Gearha Bridge fork left and drive to the road end at Tooreennahone. Park here, con-siderably.
Walk in the same direction along a rough track towards the back of the coomb which, like so many other coombs in the south-west, is called The Pocket.

4 From the top turn sharp left to descend the steep ridge to a col. Continue along the rim of the coomb to curve left to a second col. After rising from this col, a commemorative tablet can be seen. The ridge continues curving towards the south to the top of Beoun.

5 Carry on along the ridge, now descending and curving left (south east) to a col. Continue over the next top, 2096 ft (639 m), and follow the rim (now curving north-east) down into the entrance to The Pocket. Cross the stream, and regain the rough track of your outward route. Turn right and follow it back to your car.

(Map labels: Mullaghanattin 773m, B, C, 752m Beoun, The Pocket, A, Temple Dermot, Tooreennahone, P, River Blackwater, To Killarney & Sneem)

A Temple Dermot is an ancient oratory, now very ruined.

B Mullaghanattin (the hill of the gorse) is, at 2536 ft (773 m), the highest peak west of the Reeks in the Iveragh Peninsula. In addition to the distant views already mentioned, you can see, at the northern foot of the mountain, the narrow road which snakes up into the Ballaghbeama Gap – a most impressive gash in the ridge.

C Beoun, 2468 ft (752 m), is simply the anglicised version of Beann, a pointed hill. This summit has superb views over the tangle of lakes, crags, gullies and summits to the west, surely the wildest mountains in all Ireland. You can take a look at the other side of this wilderness by following Walk **22**, Coomavoher.

Walk 22
COOMAVOHER
4.5 miles (7.2 km) Easy, but rough underfoot

The MacGillycuddy's Reeks must always be the first aim of anyone who wishes to walk the Kerry Mountains, but no walker should neglect the smaller, wilder, mountains further west in the Iveragh Peninsula. The wild, boggy, craggy and trackless lake-filled coombs above the Inny Valley do not offer easy walking, *except* in Coomavoher, where for quite a small output of energy, the walker can get close-up views of one of the finest mountain valleys in Kerry.

4 *Your return is by the outward route.*

1 *From Waterville, take the road north of Lough Currane, heading for Derriana Lough. After about 8 miles (12.9 km) fork right along the north shore of Derriana Lough. The road deteriorates as it climbs the slopes above the lake, and ends beside a new bungalow, where there is space to park.*
Walking 50 yards (46 m) back, an old bog road will take you, almost dryshod, to Lough Tooreenbog. The track peters out, so keep along the south side of the lake, following the occasional sheep track.

2 *At the second lake, Lough Adoolig, there is a small cliff on the south shore, which is avoided by climbing 100 feet (30 m) or so over a small shoulder, and descending to the shore.*

3 *Go past the third, very small lake, to the fourth, keeping always to the south shore. At the far end of the fourth lake, the cliffs rise abruptly all around.*

A This walk combines beautiful views with a very pleasant example of a glaciated valley. Notice how the ice has truncated all the overlapping spurs which are such a feature of water-cut valleys.

B Geologists call a string of small lakes in a valley like this 'Paternoster Lakes', and the five in this valley (the fifth is beyond the scope of this walk) are as fine a set of prayer beads (prayer beads are known as a paternoster) as you will find in nature. Such lakes are typical of glacial valleys, overdeepened by ice.

C As you come round the foot of the spur to the fourth lake you see the abrupt end of the valley in a cirque of purple and brown sandstone cliffs, dropping directly into the lake. On the right is a waterfall coming down from a hidden upper coomb, which cradles the fifth lake. Such a formation, a relic of a time when the ice in the lower valley was many hundred feet thick, is called a 'hanging valley'. Notice also the smooth, and sometimes striated surface of the rocks, worn by stones frozen into the glacier.

COAD

2.5 miles (4 km) Easy

Part of this walk is on The Kerry Way long distance footpath, marked with yellow arrows and the sign of a walking man. There are splendid views across the Kenmare River. The circular walk described here can be extended by continuing along the Old Road as far as the mountain ridge at Windy Gap, which is 2 miles (3.2 km) further up. This section of the Old Road can be found easily.

1 *Leave the N70 Ring of Kerry road about 1 mile (1.6 km) west of Castlecove, turning towards the mountain (signposted 'Kerry Walking Route'). Follow the small road for 2 miles (3.2 km) to the car park space below the modern graveyard.*
On leaving the car, join the Old Road at the T-junction. This is part of The Kerry Way. The ruined church is seen on your right. Turn left after a stream. The road goes straight ahead as a rough track and can be clearly seen between walls. Stiles give access over fences.

5 *The track leads down until it reaches a ruined dwelling house. Enter the small road through double gates, closing them behind you. Turn right down the bohereen (lane) which leads downwards and westwards. The lane continues back to the starting point.*

4 *From this gate the track is obscure. In a few yards turn sharp left, then sharp right between two small hills. Regain the view of the sea and there the grassy track becomes clear on the left.*

3 *At this point there is a gate in the fence on the right (the seaward side). The Old Road is seen ahead, crossing two streams; white marks on the hill above indicate the copper mines. Turn right through this gate and secure it.*

2 *At this point the walls are left behind, and the road is on the open mountain. The medicinal plant Camomile is abundant underfoot. The road ahead comes from Caherdaniel, 1 mile (1.6 km) distant. Turn right up the stony track, from which there is a splendid panoramic view.*

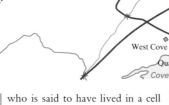

A Kilcrohane Church gives its name to the present parish of Kilcrohane, although the building was already a ruin by 1750. The graveyard now extends to the hill opposite. There is a Holy Well associated with Saint Crohane, who is said to have lived in a cell near the Copper Mines. The Saint's day is 29th July.

B The circular outline of a ring fort is just discernible when seen from the footpath higher up.

C This is the site of copper mines, although few signs can now be seen on the surface. The mines were last worked in the 17th century. Tested again about 1900, they were finally abandoned.

0 _____ 1 mile
0 _____ 1 km

This is a varied walk through woodland, shore and mountain vegetation, which begins in the old woods around Derrynane House. The route follows the Mass Path, which was much used to and from church, before the advent of the motor car. The hill is climbed by road to about 400 feet (122 m) to join the Old Road. There are discerned, rising steeply up the hill on the left, grass covered between overgrown walls and lined with wooden poles carrying cables. Follow this route.

extensive views of Kenmare Bay, the islands and the distant coast of Cork. The return to Derrynane House is by a road along the woodland margin.

6 *Keeping on the stony road, cross a stream where a path comes down from the Scariff Inn. Pass through a gate and secure it. In the next hollow the Old Road can be*

5 *At this point the road takes a sharp left turn. Leave the road and take a rough stony road to the right.*

4 *The houses of Bealtra and Bunavalla are below, and there is a good view of the harbour. There is a dwelling house on the right just before the turn.*

3 *The path crosses the shore to the pier at Bealtra, opposite the harbour entrance. Follow the road up the hill.*

2 *Behind a building, once a boathouse, turn right along the Mass Path. This winds among the rocks along the coast and care must be taken when the rocks are wet and slippery.*

7 *After a steep zigzag, the Old Road becomes more obvious (poles with two heavy cables mark the route). There are panoramic views here. Cross the wall blocking the road and pass the sheltered valley with holly and alder trees.*

8 *Follow the poles. The track takes a sharp right turn at the top of the hill towards the wall of the Dunraven estate. Turn left beside this wall.*

9 *On reaching the tarred road, turn right to return to Derrynane House, about 0.5 mile (0.8 km) below.*

To Kenmare

Derrynane Harbour
Pier
Hotel
Lodge
Derrynane House

Abbey Island

Derrynane Bay

1 *Start from Derrynane House, which is signposted to the left 1.5 miles (2.4 km) to the west of Caherdaniel, on the N70 Ring of Kerry road 18.5 miles (30 km) from Kenmare. There is a car park.*

Leave Derrynane House by woodland path to the Lodge, then turn left along the road to the pier. Alternatively walk all the way to the pier along the sandy shore when the tide is low.

A Derrynane House was the ancestral home of the Liberator, Daniel O'Connell (1775-1847). He was the first great leader of Catholic Irish democracy, and was elected to the House of Commons in 1829. Derrynane House is open to the public.

B Derrynane Pier and Harbour. In the past there was extensive traffic with France, Spain and Portugal.

C This woodland is part of the private estate of the Earl of Dunraven.

GOUGANE BARRA
7 miles (11.3 km) Strenuous (see page 8)

The Lee, for most of its length a gentle river, and tamed to provide hydro-electric power, rises in magnificent Wagnerian scenery at Gougane Barra. To be exact, this is the name of the lake in the Coomroe Glen, but popularly the whole valley is known as Gougane Barra. Near the Kerry border, at the eastern end of the Caha Mountains, Coomroe is a magnificent glacial cirque, with the moraine-dammed lake nestling below dark sandstone crags, and the rest of the glen floor clothed in conifers. A favourite spot for 19th-century tourists, it has been drawn, painted, and photographed from every imaginable angle, but it has sufficient beauty to rise above its popularity. The early Church in Ireland tended to search out remote places, and St Finbar is reputed to have built a monastery on Holy Island in the lake in the 6th century. Coomroe is also called 'deep valley Desmond', recalling the name of the Norman-Irish family which ruled nearly all Munster in the late Middle Ages.

The walk rises above the crags surrounding the valley to give splendid views; both close and distant, but it must be stressed that *once commenced, the walk cannot easily be abandoned*, except by retracing your steps. However, this need not deter you from a visit. If the weather is not suitable for a high-level walk, there are short walks laid out by the Forestry Service around the lake and in the forested glen. Information about these walks can be obtained on the spot.

A Inchigeelagh, on the approach road, has long been a favourite haunt of artists. Ballingeary is a popular centre for studying the Irish language.

B The buildings on Holy Island are generally credited with a greater age than they are due. Nothing remains of St Finbar's monastery, which was probably simply built of wattle-and-daub, or at most comprised stone beehive huts.

The small church was built in 1900, and had for its inspiration Cormac's Chapel on the Rock of Cashel. It has some fine stained glass. The square stone court nearby was built by Father Denis O'Mahony at the end of the 17th century. In the centre of the court is a platform with a wooden cross, inscribed in Latin, Irish and English 'Here stood in the sixth century, the cell of St Finbar, first bishop of Cork'. On the walls of the court are a fine set of terracotta Stations of the Cross, now unfortunately rather damaged. Father O'Mahony lived and died on the island.

C This track is the only feasible break in the cliffs surrounding the upper end of the valley. Known as Poll (the hole) it has long been an escape route in time of trouble, most recently during the War of Independence in 1920-21. It was also used by pilgrims, and probably funerals, coming to Gougane from the Borlin Valley to the west.

D To the north-west Corrán Tuathail (see Walk **17**) can now be seen, with Caher on its left. The Borlin Valley lies below and on the left again the Caha Mountains, beyond Glengariff, extend into the Beara Peninsula.

E Lough Fadda is perched curiously on top of the ridge below you. To the west, Caoinkeen (Akinkeen) stands out boldly, whilst Mangerton Mountain (see Walk **11**) lies to the north-west. The Paps (see Walk **7**) can just be seen to the north.

F There is a fine view here across the coomb to the cliffs on the north side. A cross or T-shaped mark can be seen on the rock, indicating a hiding place once used by men 'on the run'. The mountain behind is called Bealick, probably from the Irish, béal lice, mouth of a rock (ie. a cave). There are views to the south and south-west over Bantry Bay, and the ill-fated Oil Terminal on Whiddy Island.

Over

GOUGANE BARRA

Continued

2 Take the path which leaves the road here and immediately crosses a wooden bridge, to follow a signpost for Slí Sléibhe. After about 225 yards (206 m), at another signpost, fork right and wind your way up through the forest to emerge above. Leave the path at once, climbing straight up the rough grassy slope for 0.5 mile (0.8 km) until you are above the level of the cliffs to your left. Then turn left (south-west), ascending more gently, to join the wide and level ridge above.

3 Veer slightly left and continue for about 0.5 mile (0.8 km) until a small lake is seen below to the left, and shortly afterwards a large lake on the col below. Descend quite steeply on rough ground to the right of the second lake.

1 From Cork follow the N22, turning left 1 mile (1.6 km) before Macroom on the R584 for Inchigeelagh and Ballingeary. Approximately 3 miles (4.8 km) beyond Ballingeary turn right for the Gougane Barra Hotel, which is on the left near the end of the lake. The walk begins at the car park there.

Turn left along the road, shortly reaching the causeway to Holy Island. Beyond this continue for 1.5 miles (2.4 km) on the main asphalt road past two car parks with toilets to another car park at the head of the valley, where the road turns sharply back.

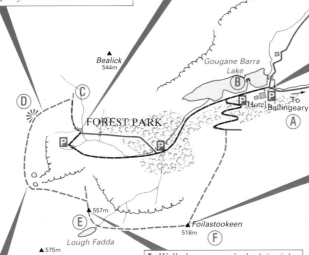

6 Turn left from the narrow ridge ahead to descend along a broad ridge (in a north-east direction). This ridge leads down to the forest below, with one short steep section best taken on the right. After a level section of coarse grass veer left to reach and cross the forest fence. Maintain your direction (north) to reach a forest road which zigzags back down to the asphalt road by the lake. Turn right to return to your parked car.

4 From the second lake veer left again, crossing a wire fence, until a fine outcrop of rock is seen ahead. This is passed on the right. On reaching the ridge above, walk to your left briefly to get a fine view of Gougane Barra. Then turn around to walk to the minor summit at 1828 ft (557 m) overlooking Lough Fadda.

5 Walk down towards the left of the lake, and then veer to the left (south-east) until a wire fence is met. Follow the fence until it turns to the right. Leave the fence and carry straight on for 225 yards (206 m) more to gain the top of Foilastookeen (the cliff of the little pinnacle), 1698 ft (518 m).

BARLEY LAKE

6 miles (9.7 km) Strenuous (see page 8)

The north-west corner of Bantry Bay is warm, sheltered and studded with islands. At its head is the pleasant and popular village of Glengarriff. Inland to the west and high up, Barley Lake lies in a horseshoe of fine ridges and wild moorland, with deep-cut valleys beyond these ridges to the north and south. This walk takes you round the horseshoe. There are changes in mood as the focus of interest moves away from the lake to the distant scene, then to the lonely moorland and finally to the breathtaking south ridge. The going is at times rough although the ground is well drained. Save this walk for a fine, clear day. **Do not undertake this walk in misty conditions**.

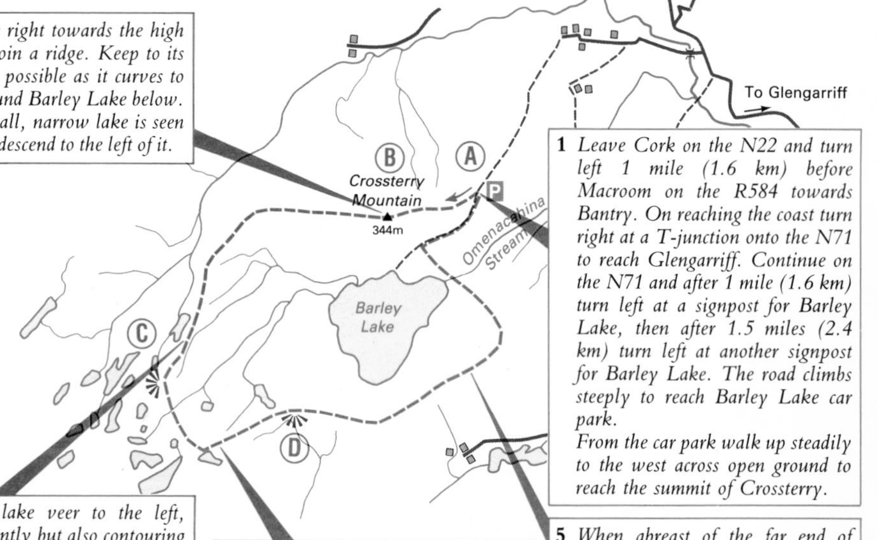

2 *Veer to the right towards the high ground to join a ridge. Keep to its crest where possible as it curves to the left around Barley Lake below. When a small, narrow lake is seen on the left, descend to the left of it.*

1 *Leave Cork on the N22 and turn left 1 mile (1.6 km) before Macroom on the R584 towards Bantry. On reaching the coast turn right at a T-junction onto the N71 to reach Glengarriff. Continue on the N71 and after 1 mile (1.6 km) turn left at a signpost for Barley Lake, then after 1.5 miles (2.4 km) turn left at another signpost for Barley Lake. The road climbs steeply to reach Barley Lake car park.*
From the car park walk up steadily to the west across open ground to reach the summit of Crossterry.

3 *From the lake veer to the left, climbing gently but also contouring to some extent, for about 1 mile (1.6 km), going to the left of a larger lake to reach the ridge overlooking the Coomarkane Valley far below.*

4 *Walk along the ridge, keeping to the crest where possible. Steep sections are best passed on the left. Later, the ground steepens on the left over Barley Lake and your descent can be made to the right.*

5 *When abreast of the far end of Barley Lake, leave the ridge and walk to the start of the exit stream. Walk across the stream and take the track which forks right (north-west) from the shoreline and climbs slightly. After about 450 yards (411 m) – pace this out to avoid an overshoot – a faint fisherman's track comes up from the lake. Follow this to the right through peat hag to reach the crest, and return to the car park.*

A The road discreetly stops short of the final crest to leave the lake in placid solitude. Walk up to the crest and notice the fishermen's track down to the lake. This will have to be picked up on your return. Note the curious deep parallel channels in some of the rocks – probably selective weathering rather than a glacial effect.

B Pause on top of Crossterry Mountain to enjoy the view to the east over Bantry Bay, then south to the steep face of Sugarloaf Mountain (see Walk **27**). Further round to the west there is the long line of the Caha Mountains.

C Attractive small scale scenery of moorland, rock, lakes and streams.

D A splendid view of the sweep down to Lough Nambrack and the Coomarkane Valley.

Map labels: To Glengarriff · B · A · P · Crossterry Mountain · 344m · Omenachina Stream · Barley Lake · C · D

SUGARLOAF MOUNTAIN

3 miles (4.8 km) Moderate (see page 8)

This fine mountain to the south-west of Glengarriff commands attention, with a magnificent summit ridge which ends suddenly at the summit point. A moderately steep ascent is made on firm grassy slopes with occasional rock and heather higher up. The descent on the longer western flank is a joy.

4 Now climb straight up (north) across open country, aiming for the high ground above. Near the top, skirt around steep ground on the right, and soon the summit ridge is reached. Turn right over innumerable little tops to reach the real summit. You will know for sure when you get there!

5 Return along the ridge and stay on it veering a little to the left until a large col appears below, with a wide grassy valley to the left. Go down to the head of the valley and descend on the far side of the main stream. When you are near the improved pasture below, swing left (south-east) to join a track. Go left along this track, which leads to the gate in the wire fence, which you used on the ascent. Go down the field and go right, then left, to reach the bohereen and the main road.

3 Go through the gate and turn right and right again, following the fence on another grass road which finally expires on a broad mountain road. Follow this road up to the left and round a hairpin bend. Leave it on the left after 300 yards (274 m) when it begins to descend.

2 Follow the grass road to the right until it stops at a field. Cross a small ditch into the field and turn up left alongside a wire fence until a gate is reached on the left.

1 Leave Cork on the N22 and turn left 1 mile (1.6 km) before Macroom on the R584. At the coast take the N71 for Glengarriff and turn left there on the R572 towards Castletown Berehaven. After 4 miles (6.4 km) and just short of a large white house with a signpost for Zetland pier beyond, turn right. After 1.5 miles (2.4 km) there are two farmhouses quite close on the right, and two roads up to them. Park on the roadside near the second road.
Walk up the second road and turn left at the top to follow briefly a bohereen (a lane) which turns right and ends in rough pasture land. Continue upwards. Very shortly, a grass road is met.

A Choose any direction or just look straight down and you have a view to marvel at. To the west across the Adrigole Valley there is the craggy mass of Hungry Hill (see Walk **28**). The last and highest of the chain of the Caha Mountains is on its right. Beyond, there are glimpses of the peaks of the Iveragh Peninsula. A splendid wilderness landscape lies below, whilst beyond Glengarriff there are the fine hills of west Cork. Finally to the south a lovely spread of islands can be seen, hopefully in a glittering Bantry Bay, with Mount Gabriel (see Walk **32**) beyond.

Walk 28

HUNGRY HILL

6.5 miles (10.5 km) Strenuous (see page 8)

The summit of Hungry Hill, at 2248 ft (685 m), is the highest point on the Beara Peninsula, and makes a fine, energetic walk. The mountain provided an appropriately brooding, if distant, background to the Daphne du Maurier novel of the same name. Some say it was once called Angry Hill, and not without reason, for it is a massive craggy mountain with a large exposed summit plateau and a fortress aspect from the south. The route goes up through these ramparts using a trail marked out, curiously, for visiting groups of Belgian youngsters. Red markers on the rocks are often faded, so it is better to rely on route-finding judgement over the rugged ground on the back ridge from the summit to the green road. **Do not undertake this walk if you are unsure of your route-finding ability**.

Hungry Hill

A A short breather here is justified by the pleasant view unfolding below. Bear (or Bere) Island lying off the coast has Martello towers on the central ridge and a sizeable fort. There is even an admiral's house, for this was once a large British naval base. Mount Gabriel (see Walk **31**) can be seen to the left across Bantry Bay.

B This breezy spot gives a splendid view south over the islands of Bantry Bay. Cape Clear Island (see Walk **31**) can be seen beyond Mount Gabriel, and to the right again the Fastnet Rock is visible. To the north and west all the major peaks of the Killarney region and the Iveragh Peninsula are revealed.

C Both sides of the ridge are laced with crags, so keep to the recommended route.

D This rugged but attractive ridge separates Cork (to the south) from Kerry. Looking north-east along the sombre Glanmore Valley, Glanmore Lake can be seen, beyond which Cummeengeera (see Walk **29**) comes down from the left.

Over

0   1 mile
0   1 km

5 *Turn left onto the road and follow its winding course down to the main road. Turn left to return to your car.*

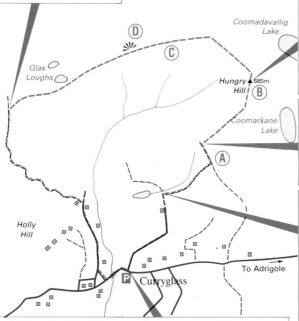

Coomadavallig Lake

Glas Loughs

Hungry ▲685m Hill Ⓑ

Ⓒ Ⓓ

Coomarkane Lake

Ⓐ

Holly Hill

To Adrigole

Ⓟ Curryglass

4 *Continue in the same direction (north) for about 200 yards (183 m) to avoid crags before bearing left (north-west) for about 700 yards (640 m) down a broad ridge, and then bearing left again (due west) for much the same distance on or near the ill-defined crest of the ridge. One of the Glas Loughs can be seen ahead. The course just gently curves to the left to pass to the left of the lough. Continue on much the same course crossing a shallow valley. Shortly a good green road is joined.*

3 *Climb up this gully maintaining the same course (slightly north of east), as it crosses other openings. When the summit plateau is gained, walk to the left (north) to the high ground. Continue on to reach the summit survey point.*

2 *Continue ahead on a faint track which soon veers left (north-east) with a stream on the left. The stream disappears off to the left and in a short while a green road is reached. Follow this to the left, and as it dies continue climbing to the left (north-west) up a grassy slope for a short while, until an opening appears on the right. Walk up this to reach a grassy platform with an obvious gully continuing above.*

1 *Leave Cork on the N22 and turn left 1 mile (1.6 km) before Macroom on the R584. At the coast turn right on the N71 for Glengarriff and turn left there on the R572 signposted 'Castletown Berehaven'. It is 11 miles (17.7 km) to the village of Adrigole and, after a further 5 miles (8 km),* *there is a minor asphalt road to the right with a signpost for Hungry Hill. Park near this junction. Walk up the road and through a gate to the crest of the hill. When the lake is seen below, walk on for about 100 yards (91 m) and turn off right at a rock with a painted red marker.*

Walk 29
CUMMEENGEERA
2.5 miles (4 km) Easy

The Beara summits, often boggy and uninteresting plateaux, cannot compare with those of the MacGillycuddy's Reeks, and the area as a whole takes second place to the nearby Iveragh Peninsula. But the valleys and coombs are some of the finest in Kerry. This walk, in Cummeengeera, 'the sheeps' pasture', offers a pleasant stroll up a typical Beara valley.

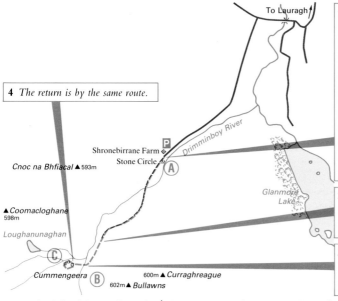

4 *The return is by the same route.*

Shronebirrane Farm
Stone Circle
Cnoc na Bhfiacal ▲ 593m

▲ Coomacloghane
598m

Loughanunaghan

Cummengeera

600m ▲ Curraghreague
602m ▲ Bullawns

Drimminboy River

Glanmore Lake

To Lauragh

1 *From Kenmare take the R571 to Lauragh. In the village turn left up the pleasant wooded by-road towards Glanmore Lake. After about 0.75 mile (1.2 km) take a right turn, cross the bridge across the Cluanshagh River, and after 0.5 mile (0.8 km) turn left up a lane. Leave your car considerably parked where the surfacing ends, just near a farm (Shronebirrane). Follow the road, which becomes a rough track, crosses the stream, and dies out below Bullawns (also known as Lackabane).*

2 *Continue walking parallel to the stream to just beyond a point where another small stream joins it from the right.*

3 *Cross the Drimminboy River easily and continue straight ahead to arrive at the ruins of a 19th-century village.*

A On the left of the road are the remains of a stone circle. If you wish to visit it, please ask at the farm, since it is not a National Monument. There is also an earth ringfort on the lower slopes across the river.

B This is a typical glacial coomb, with a 'hanging valley' containing a small lake, Loughanunaghan, up to the right. It is a magnificent, but daunting, valley, with great masses of dark sandstone rock broken by heavily vegetated ledges, and stained by dribbles from patches of wet moss.

C Here is a 19th-century village, with ruins of small stone cottages, and traces of fields. The rapidly increasing population at the beginning of that century forced people to inhabit such remote spots, where no road ever reached. After the famine of the 1840s, which through death or emigration halved the population, villages such as this were mostly abandoned, though a hermit still lived here 50 years ago. There is a gruesome tale also of Sean Rabach, murderer of an Englishman (probably a deserter from the nearby British Naval Base at Berehaven) who came to him for help. He was observed by a woman going early to the stream for water; sometime later she let him know what she knew, so he strangled her, and left her with her head in the stream so it appeared she had drowned. Once again he was observed, this time by a man stealing cows' tails, who told the police. However Rabach used to retreat to a high-up hidden cave, and stayed free for many years until the woman's son was grown, and helped the police to catch him one Christmas night.

Walk 30
LOUGH INE
4.5 miles (7.2 km) Easy

Lough Ine is an almost totally landlocked sea lough. It is both a geological and a zoological curiosity, as well as being a very pleasant place, with a popular picnic site. The unique feature of the lough is the tidal race which occurs four times a day through a narrow channel about a quarter of a mile (400 m) long. When this tide race is not running the lough is effectively undisturbed, as few streams supply it. The clear water reveals the exotic and colourful nature of the marine life. This includes sub-tropical species which unexpectedly thrive near the surface, even though the depth on the western side reaches 150 feet (46 m). The woods above the lough are mainly deciduous and are equally attractive (but less visited). This walk, after exploring the lough, zigzags gently up the face of the hill with excellent lookout points, particularly near the summit.

5 *Return to the fork and descend to the sign marked 'hilltop'. Turn left and descend onto a track going left. This eventually takes you to the road, which you cross to return to the car park.*

4 *Return to the fork and turn left on a lesser track winding through a small copse, shortly emerging to reach the summit.*

1 *Take the R595 road from Skibbereen towards Baltimore and turn off left after 2 miles (3.2 km) at a signpost for Lough Ine. The lough is reached in another 2 miles (3.2 km) after a steep descent. Turn left immediately for the car park 400 yards (366 m) on.*
Walk back to the main road, turn left and and walk along to where the road forks. You will return to this point later in the walk. Take the left fork and walk along the side of the sea lough.

2 *Continue for 1 mile (1.6 km) to a gate. Turn left through it and walk down to the water. Now retrace your steps to the fork in the road at the head of the lough. The forest trail begins up some steps on the left.*

3 *Walk up the track as it zigzags through the forest, and note a sign marked 'hilltop' for the descent. Carry on up eventually passing through a gap in a wall. When you are near the top, fork left for an excellent viewpoint.*

To Baltimore

E
198m▲
P
Lough Ine
Castle Island
B
D
C
81m▲
155m▲
A
F
Bullock Island

A The rapids are at their most turbulent at half-tide, especially during spring tides (which occur every two weeks just after the time of the new and full moon).

B The ruins of Cloghan Castle can be seen on the island. This area was once an O'Driscoll stronghold.

C The information board gives well-illustrated examples of the more exotic creatures in the lake. Please note that it is forbidden to collect shell-fish from the lough.

D Sherkin and Cape Clear (see Walk 31) islands are not far off to the south-west. Beyond and to their right is the picturesque port of Crookhaven, with Mizen Head (see Walk 33) at the end of the peninsula.

E To the north-west Mount Gabriel (see Walk 32) is easily recognised by its tracking station on top. Bantry Bay lies beyond to its right.

F A pleasant and very sheltered anchorage, but a hazardous passage to the exit of the lough. Bullock Island is joined to the mainland by a causeway which is covered at high tide.

Walk 31
CAPE CLEAR ISLAND

2.5 miles (4 km) Easy

Cape Clear Island, the birth place of St Ciárán, is situated 7 miles (11.3 km) south of Baltimore. This walk covers the centre of the island and includes a variety of interesting places to visit and stunning panoramic views. It is by no means the only possible route on the island, but it is a very good appetiser. The 140 inhabitants of this Gaeltacht (Irish speaking) island will gladly point you in the right direction for those sites not included, such as the druidic standing stones and Loch Ioral.

4 *EITHER* *continue along this road which brings you back down into North Harbour, **OR** just over the hill past the goat farm you will see a stone gate on your left. Climb over the adjacent stone stile and follow the footpath. The last 100 yards (91 m) of this path are very steep.*

5 *The path brings you down next to a corner shop. Turn right to return to North Harbour.*

1 *Cape Clear Island is 7 miles (11.3 km) south of Baltimore, and is reached by regular ferry from Schull and Baltimore. Ring the island co-op on 028 39119 for details of sailing times. The ferry delivers you to North Harbour. Turn right at the end of the pier, take the first left fork and St Ciáráns church is on your right. Retrace your steps and take the road up the hill, keeping left, following signs to the youth hostel.*

2 *Just before the youth hostel, take the turning to your left.*

3 *Just after the lane to the Post Office there is a stone stile on your left. Climb over it and follow the path until you come out next to the church. Turn left and walk along the road.*

A St Ciárán was born on the island in AD 352. This church dates back to the 12th century but there is evidence that it stands on the site of an earlier building reputed to have been built by St Ciárán himself.

B Note the Napoleonic watch tower on the hill to your right. Built between 1798 and 1806 against the threat of a French invasion, it was declared a national monument in 1989. It stands next to the original island lighthouse built in 1817 but which proved to be ineffective in fog, and so was replaced by the lighthouse on the Fastnet Rock in 1854. The tower and old lighthouse are both accessible by road.

C Before 1971 there was no electricity on the island. Now, 70% of the island's needs are supplied by one of the most sophisticated wind generating systems in the world. The site of the windmills is thought by many archaeologists to be a Megalithic passage grave (so called because a passage leads from the outside of the tumulus to the burial chamber within), and at one time a leprosy quarantine for suspected sufferers sailing into the port of Baltimore. At 533 feet (163 m) above sea level, it is the highest point on the island.

D The Heritage Centre is open to the public most afternoons from June to the end of August, but may be visited all through the year by arrangement.

E The goat farm sells a range of goatsmilk products, including ice-cream.

F This point commands a view of the Fastnet Rock Lighthouse and Dún An Óir Castle, 'The Fort of Gold'. Built by the O'Driscoll pirates around 1450, it has a colourful history of battles and sieges. In the 1700's it was the home of Concubhar Mac Eireamhain, the Cape Clear giant who was over 8 feet (2.4 m) tall and lived here as a hermit. The present lighthouse first shone in July 1904 and was manned until automated in 1989.

MOUNT GABRIEL

4 miles (6.4 km) Moderate

0   1 mile

0   1 km

Despite its modest height of 1335 ft (407 m), Mount Gabriel dominates the whole of the surrounding region. It can be identified from afar by the two shiny spheres of the tracking station on top. The walk reaches a fine viewpoint on the summit ridge south of the station. The ascent is a little rough but it starts high and, if you take care, it is tolerably dry. The return by the access road is a gentle refreshing stroll with a wide panoramic scene of great variety.

4 *Return to the access road and descend along it to the public road below. Turn right and right again, to walk back to your car.*

1 *Leave Cork on the N71 to Skibbereen and Ballydehob, then take the R592 towards Schull. About 1 mile (1.6 km) short of Schull turn right towards Durrus. After 2 miles (3.2 km) a craggy col is reached. Park the car on the roadside beyond the brow of the hill.*
Walk back to the brow, and on for 250 yards (228 m) to the end of the crag, to reach a grassy bank on the right. Step a few paces from the road to reach a grassy ride which begins to rise steadily to the right and reaches the ridge above the starting point.

2 *Climb up the ridge for about 0.75 mile (1.2 km), veering to the left (west), to reach the road just below the tracking station.*

3 *Cross the road and avoid boggy ground by aiming a little to the right of the right hand corner of the perimeter fence. After the corner continue close to the fence until it turns left. Carry straight on along the ridge. When a small lake appears, continue along the ridge above it to reach a small conical peak.*

▲407m
Mount Gabriel

Tracking
Station

To Schull

A The view encompasses wild hilly country, with evidence on the flank of Mount Gabriel of Neolithic copper mining, and pleasant rolling pastoral scenery.

B Beyond the attractive little sea port of Schull lie the islands of Sherkin and Cape Clear (see Walk **31**), together with a host of lesser islands. The Fastnet lighthouse may also be discernible.

C Seefin and Caher mountains can be seen to the west, beyond Dunmanus Bay. To the north and further away Sugarloaf and Hungry Hill (see Walks **27** & **28**) are visible across Bantry Bay.

MIZEN HEAD TO BARLEY COVE

0   1 mile
0   1 km

9 miles (14.5 km) Easy, but a low tide is required at Barley Cove

Barley Cove and Mizen Head are linked by an elevated coastal road which offers fine views across the bay towards Brow Head. Beyond Mizen Head a section of this walk provides easy walking on a faint grassy track, with more exciting views. Barley Cove requires a low tide when fording the stream, and you should check locally regarding this. Pleasant stretches of grassland and beach are followed by a visit to a small headland overlooking the Cove. The return walk avoids the ford and leads back to the approach road from Goleen, near which lie the ruins of an early church.

4 *At the end of the asphalt climb up ahead and to the right on a narrow track. When it divides, take the faint coastal track to the right. After 0.5 mile (0.8 km), at a huge cleft, walk up to the right to a fence coming in from the right. Walk carefully between the fence and the cliff edge to reach the crest of the ridge, where the fence turns away to the right. Enjoy the views to seaward. Return to the Barley Cove Hotel.*

Clochane

Barley Cove

Mizen Head

3 *Walk along the main road to another car park, and continue beyond the barrier towards the lighthouse.*

1 *Leave Cork on the N71 to Skibbereen and Ballydehob, then take the R592 to Schull and the R591 to Goleen. Turn right in Goleen for Barley Cove and after 4 miles (6.4 km) you pass a tidal lough. Turn left at a signpost for Mizen Head. Carry on for a short way to the car park of the Barley Cove Hotel, which is on the left. This is the start of the walk.*

Cross the car park and walk down the grassy slope to the left to emerge on the sandy foreshore by the stream. At low tide, find a good place to cross. Wade carefully across, heading diagonally right to reach the road on the other side.

2 *Turn right and follow the road to its high point on a headland by the side of the bay. Enjoy the view. Retrace your steps for a short way, but stay on the road to cross the bridge. Turn left and walk for about 0.5 mile (0.8 km) to turn left again.*

A The stream is usually less than 20 inches (51 cm) deep for an hour either side of low tide. A stick comes in handy, for testing the depth as you wade across.

B This road leads briefly inland to reach a long narrow inlet of the sea. The quaint little port of Crookhaven stands near the seaward end, on the right. To the left, near the top of the Arduslough Hills, there is a lake above which many Neolithic wedge tombs have been found.

C The fragmentary remains of the 11th-century Kilmoe church indicate that it was one of the few in west Cork in Romanesque style.

D Mizen Head is the most southerly point of the Irish mainland. Cape Clear Island (see Walk 31) and the Fastnet Rock are not far away to the east. A short distance inland there is an old watch tower and high on Mizen Peak a well-built and very large cairn of uncertain age.

E After the awesome chasm a vantage point at last reveals Three Castle Head across Dunlough Bay below. The Head is named after the great O'Mahoney fortress. Built in 1205, it is the earliest in west Cork and one of the best preserved.

KILWORTH MOUNTAINS
3.5 miles (5.6 km) Easy

This walk starts at the lonely Mountain Barracks Inn, pleasantly situated at a crossroads near the head of a wooded valley. This valley climbs gently up to the summit ridge at the eastern end of the Kilworth Mountains – a modest 978 ft (298 m) high. The walk makes some use of quiet country roads, but for the most part crosses forest land on roads and a well-defined track which can, in places, be muddy. There are splendid views – first of the Galty Mountains to the north, then of the Kilworth moorland and later of the highlands to the east. Local stories include that of Willy Brennan, the highwayman remembered in a famous song, and also Brian Boru, the great Munster King who defeated the Vikings not far down the Araglin road. The moor is often used as a firing range and the forest is within the danger area, so **do not walk here when you see the red flag**.

3 *Follow this track onto the ridge, then down and up a little until it winds to the left (south), above Kilworth moor on the right, and joins a forest road.*

4 *Continue straight on along this road until another wider road is met. Turn left and follow this to the main road. Turn left to return to the Mountain Barracks Inn.*

2 *Pass the first forest road on the left and take the second. It is about 0.5 mile (0.8 km) from the inn. About 300 yards (274 m) from the main road a barrier pole is reached. Turn right here on a lesser road and, after about 400 yards (366 m), turn left on a well-marked track.*

1 *Leave Cork on the N25 Waterford road and turn left after 3 miles (4.8 km) on the N8 to Dublin. About 2.5 miles (4 km) north of Fermoy turn right for Kilworth on the R667 and very shortly, in Kilworth, turn left towards Ballyporeen. After 5 miles (8 km), and just before a crossroads, the Mountain Barracks Inn is located on the right, with plenty of parking space.*
From the inn, walk along the road signposted to Mitchelstown.

A The Mountain Barracks Inn got its name from the nearby building which was a police barracks in the middle of the last century. The famous Bianconi stage-coaches came this way to Dublin, and needed protection from highwaymen such as Willy Brennan, who is reputed to have had a hideout hereabouts.

B The rolling Galty Mountains are some of Ireland's highest. Galtymore rises to 3015 ft (919 m).

C The firing range is well to the west. It was opened in 1896 when war with South Africa was looming and it was discovered that Boer irregulars were better marksmen than British soldiers.

D The pleasant open moorland to the east leads up to Knockshanahullion at the western end of the Knockmealdown Mountains, in county Waterford.

Walk 35

NAGLE MOUNTAINS

8 miles (12.9 km) Moderate – muddy in places

Ballyhooly Castle stands above a pleasant open stretch of the Blackwater River. The castle keep is still occupied but is all that now remains. Standing by a five-way road junction (at which *none* of the roads has priority) at the foot of the Nagle Mountains is the Castle Tavern, remarkable in that it was rebuilt at the expense of the British Government after being burnt down during the troubles surrounding the independence struggle in the early 1920s. The Nagle Mountains would be more aptly described as hills, for they are gentle and of no great height. Neolithic ring forts are numerous in the area but are difficult to locate. The walk is varied and exhilarating with forest trails, hilltop views, heather moorland and an open and effortless descent to the Blackwater Valley. The route relies on wide tracks with three lengths of little used public road. There are three short muddy sections.

Ballyhooly Castle

A Shortly before reaching the hilltop and a few paces to the left of the path there is a cairn above a heather-covered mound. This marks the site of a Neolithic grave, as does the fine cairn on the northern hilltop.

B The northern hilltop is the best viewpoint on the walk. To the north-east is Galtymore, and to the right of this the Knockmealdown Mountains rise up above and beyond Kilworth Mountains (see Walk **34**). To the west, Mount Hillary can be seen in the distance beyond the westernmost Nagles Mountains.

Over

5 Return to the track and continue down, following the track to the right at the end of the forest. After a short distance the track turns left through a gate to join a green road which leads down to the left and continues straight on over a gravel ditch. Follow the often muddy section off to the right past a farm. Continue over a low barrier. After a short while a public road is reached. Turn right along it to return to the Castle Tavern.

0 _____ 1 mile
0 _____ 1 km

Ballyhooly

Ballyhooly Castle

Ballydague

NAGLE

(A)(B)
▲ 408m

MOUNTAINS

(A)
428m ▲ Knocknaskagh

1 Leave Cork on the N25 Waterfort road, turning left after 3 miles (4.8 km) on the N8 to Fermoy, then left out of the town on the N72 Mallow road. At Ballyhooly, turn left over the bridge and park at the Castle Tavern.
Start walking up the hill by the inn for a short distance to reach a forest road on the right.

2 Beyond a barrier pole choose the left-most of three paths to start walking parallel to the road along an avenue of trees to reach a T-junction. Turn right and follow the road to an unsecured five-barred gate leading onto a green road which is followed to the left until it finally emerges on the public road. Turn right up the hill for 1 mile (1.6 km) until another forest road is reached on the right.

4 Continue along the track and after about 700 yards (640 m) fork right. This track curls round until it leads directly to the cairned summit. After a slight descent, a small lake is reached, and then a forest with a wire fence on the left. Continue to the highest point on the track and then strike off right on easy heather for the summit.

3 Turn right up the forest road, then left after a short distance onto another road which climbs steadily until it emerges above the forest and reaches a crossroads. Turn left going steeply uphill on a rough track which soon improves. A cairn is passed on the left and shortly the summit cairn and trig point are reached.

Walk 36
MULLAGHANISH MOUNTAIN
6 miles (9.7 km) Easy

This walk starts high and mainly follows little-used asphalt roads. The summit of Mullaghanish at 2123 feet (647 m) is reached on the road to the television masts. Later a farm access road is used. The distant views are good and the local scene down towards Ballyvourney is a delight. The approach drive by Glendav should not be missed and in Ballyvourney itself there is much of interest. Many of the local people speak Irish and it is a centre for studying the language. The An Mhuileann is a fine old inn.

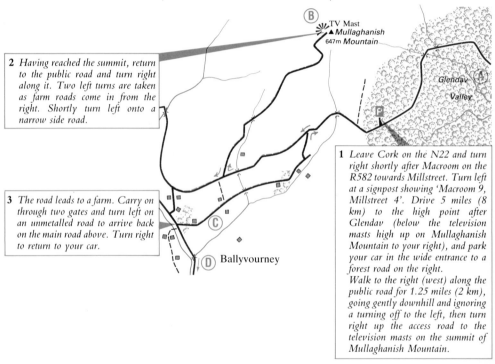

2 *Having reached the summit, return to the public road and turn right along it. Two left turns are taken as farm roads come in from the right. Shortly turn left onto a narrow side road.*

3 *The road leads to a farm. Carry on through two gates and turn left on an unmetalled road to arrive back on the main road above. Turn right to return to your car.*

1 *Leave Cork on the N22 and turn right shortly after Macroom on the R582 towards Millstreet. Turn left at a signpost showing 'Macroom 9, Millstreet 4'. Drive 5 miles (8 km) to the high point after Glendav (below the television masts high up on Mullaghanish Mountain to your right), and park your car in the wide entrance to a forest road on the right.*
Walk to the right (west) along the public road for 1.25 miles (2 km), going gently downhill and ignoring a turning off to the left, then turn right up the access road to the television masts on the summit of Mullaghanish Mountain.

A The Glendav Valley below is an attractive little punchbowl, although the effect has been diminished by an excess of conifers.

B There is a fine close-up view of the Paps (see Walk **7**) to the north-west, over in Kerry. To the west there is a distant glimpse of Glenflesk and the Killarney region, with the MacGillycuddy's Reeks beyond Mangerton Mountain (see Walk **11**).

C This lane has the simple charm of an old Irish bohereen.

D St Gobnait lived around the 6th century. She is the patron saint of the district and her bowl is still cemented to the church wall in Ballyvourney. There is a traditional story that the bowl destroyed an enemy fort when she threw it, and it then came back to her like a boomerang. The Holy Well nearby is a place of pilgrimage.

MUSHERAMORE MOUNTAIN
3.5 miles (5.6 km) Moderate

Musheramore, at 2118 ft (646 m), is the highest of the Boggeragh Mountains, which extend from Macroom in the south-west to Mallow in the north-east. This walk starts high and partly circuits the mountain before climbing it. A short length of public highway is followed by a good forest track in lovely open country overlooking the Blackwater Valley. This is followed by a brief climb on pleasant grassy moorland and a hillside traverse before reaching the summit. The descent is short and steep. The changing landscape and distant views are very rewarding and there are two interesting shrines. The approach road passes close to the Knocknakilla stone circle.

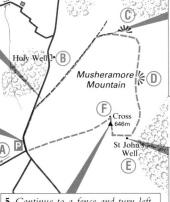

2 *Follow this over a stile and then through a gate. Go right at an obvious fork ahead and shortly the road abruptly ends.*

1 *Leave Cork on the N22 and turn right after Macroom on the R582 towards Millstreet. Fork right after 6.5 miles (10.4 km), shortly beyond Carriganimy village. After 0.75 mile (1.2 km) turn right and after 2 miles (3.2 km) turn right again at a signpost for Knocknakilla stone circle. This is seen 1 mile (1.6 km) along on the right, and beyond this there is a T-junction and sign-post. The walk starts here. Cars can be parked by the road-side.*
Walk along the Millstreet road for 700 yards (640 m), then turn right on a good forest track.

5 *Continue to a fence and turn left, descending carefully down the steep slope, with the fence on your right, to reach the road and return to your car.*

3 *Veer to the right and climb the grassy moorland until you see the wood on your left. Now traverse round the hillside and, when a white-painted cairn is seen high up towards the summit, make straight for it. This is the second Holy Well.*

4 *Ascend, maintaining your direction (west) and then, when you see it, make for the cairned cross up to your right. Then walk to the summit survey point.*

A Traces of these mysterious Celtic pre-Christian stone circles can be counted in hundreds throughout Ireland, but few are as complete as this, the Knocknakilla stone circle.

B The Holy Well by the roadside below, with the Stations of the Cross, is dedicated to St John the Baptist. There is a pattern (celebratory gathering) every 24th June. Like many other shrines it is built over an earlier holy place of pagan origin. By tradition the water provides a cure for warts.

C Galtymore is visible to the north-east. A backward glance reveals the summit of Caherbarnagh and Mullaghanish (see Walk **36**) over the valley to the west and the Paps (see Walk **7**) between them.

D There is an exhilarating view down to the Lee Valley and the reservoirs. Good walking can be found in the forest on the left but the entry points are from the road to the south.

E This was the original St John's Well and the pattern took place here until a century ago when, out of consideration for the infirm, the roadside well was built.

F Not far from the summit there is a cairn with a large cross. From the summit itself the western scene has unfolded further, with Corrán Tuathail (see Walk **17**) in the distance just to the left of the Paps. Mangerton Mountain (see Walk **11**) stands out to the right of Mullaghanish.

FOTA ISLAND

2.5 miles (4 km) Easy

The quiet and gracefully wooded island estate of Fota lies in the estuary of the River Lee alongside the northern edge of Cork harbour. The island was purchased by University College Cork in 1975 and they used most of it for experimental farming. This walk links the small but attractive Wildlife Park with the fine Regency Fota House and its impressive arboretum. A recent change of management may affect some of the details described here. If in doubt, check with the Tourism Office in Cork.

4 Immediately beyond the front of Fota House, turn left through a narrow gateway to enter the arboretum and left again to reach the back of the house. Turn right up two flights of stone steps to reach a crossing of paths.

3 Turn right on to a tarmac road and follow it to reach Fota House.

2 At the signpost beyond the cattle grid turn left and keep the grass enclosure on your left to reach the cheetah enclosures. Turn right along a forest path and ignore all turns on the left until a main track is reached, labelled 'Animal Trail'. Turn left, and then at the flamingo lake turn right onto the track signposted to the railway station. This leaves the Park at the north entrance.

5 Turn right and ignore all side paths to reach a reedy lake ahead with a small island. Turn left, and then right, following the path to the exit. The car park is ahead to your right.

1 Fota Island is 10 miles (16 km) from Cork. Take the N25 and branch right after 7 miles (11.3 km) on the road to Cobh. The estate is clearly signposted to the right, and the car park is just inside the entrance. An alternative is to take a Cobh train from Cork to Fota station, and join the walk at instruction **3**.
Walk towards the Wildlife Park, which is visible from the car park. Once inside the Park, pass the buildings on the right and then turn right on a track through open ground, keeping a low barrier to your left.

A Fota Wildlife Park has been created with care and imagination. There is a feeling of space despite its small size and varied habitat. Other paths are worth exploring, since it is always very easy to regain the recommended route. It is open from mid March to the end of October, from 11 – 6 weekdays, 2 – 6 Sundays, and on Sundays in the winter. An admission fee is charged.

B Originally an 18th-century hunting lodge, Fota House was enlarged and embellished in the 1820s in Regency style for the Smith-Barry family by the architect Sir William Morrison. The hall inside and the ground floor rooms are all impressive. There is also a fine display of large Irish landscape paintings, thanks to a co-operative effort between their owner Richard Wood and University College. The opening dates and times are those of the Wildlife Park. An admission fee is charged. Teas are available in the drawing-room.

C The arboretum has an international reputation and contains some 750 listed species or hybrids from a wide variety of temperate and subtropical regions around the world. They thrive in the mild Atlantic air and shelter provided by the surrounding land. The walk takes a central route but there is much else to see. A map is posted a few paces to the right after the entry point, and a catalogue can be purchased at Fota House.

FARRAN PARK

2 miles (3.2 km) Easy

0   1 mile
0   1 km

The pleasant winding ribbon of water south of Coachford is part of the Lee Valley reservoir. Farran Park lies along its southern bank. On the way to the sart of the walk it is worth making a short detour to the gaunt ruin of Kilcrea Abbey, which is best viewed from the charming little bridge over the River Bride. The huge skeleton of the church and massive tower remain. Many members of the McCarthy clan are buried here, as well as the outlaw hero Art O'Leary. Across the road and over a field the ruins of Kilcrea Castle stand on an ancient earthworks. Farran Park gives a very pleasant and relaxed stroll with appreciable variation in scenery. Amenities provided by the Forest and Wildlife Services include a car park, a good circuit road with additional forest tracks, a small but interesting Display Centre and a fenced off pond with mallard and other species.

1 *Leave Cork on the N22. After 11 miles (17.7 km) take a minor road to the left signposted for Kilcrea Friary. Shortly another signpost directs you to the right. You will see the Abbey before you cross the bridge over the River Bride. Carry on to the broad approach road on the left and park to visit the Abbey.*
Return to and immediately cross the N22 on a minor road with a signpost for Farran Park. Turn left at a T-junction and in less than 1 mile (1.6 km) fork right, shortly reaching Farran Park on the right. The car park is inside.
Beyond the barrier pole, walk straight along the forest road to the pond, then along the fence to the Display Centre. Continue to some sheds and turn left to reach a T-junction. Turn right and at the start of a hairpin bend go straight on, along a forest track, to reach a clearing by the water's edge.

3 *Turn right passing above the Cork Power Boat Club shed. When the road bends left at a grassy clearing ahead, go straight on along a faint track which leads to a bank above the shoreline. Carry on and rejoin the forest road. Turn right, then left, to return to the car park.*

2 *At the north edge of the clearing near the shore, a thin track climbs a bank into woodland and descends beyond. Carry straight on (not left) to pass by a rocky beach and shortly regain the main forest road. Turn right passing the Rowing Club shed to reach a T-junction.*

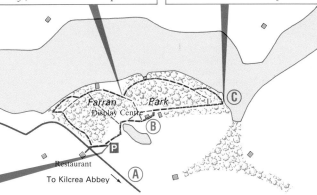

A The abbey and castle ruins stand as mute tributes to the vanished power of the McCarthy clan, like Blarney and many other picturesque ruins to the west. The two here were built in 1465 by Cormac McCarthy, Lord of Muskerry, who gave the abbey to the Franciscan Order. Religious houses were proscribed in 1542, but the abbey survived until Oliver Cromwell's ubiquitous presence resulted in its slow decay. Art O'Leary, who is buried here, was outlawed and shot in 1773. He had refused to sell his his horse, a fine hunter for £5, as the penal laws against Catholics required. At this time the Catholic community was still sorely oppressed, following William III's victory over James II at the Battle of the Boyne in 1690.

B The variety of trees in the park is well illustrated at the Display Centre. Many of these are deciduous, some are exotic and others, such as the strawberry tree, are quite weird.

C The path leads to a grassy clearing with an attractive view of nearby wooded hillsides across the water. This is followed by a delightful forest track.

OLD HEAD OF KINSALE

2 miles (3.2 km) Easy

Kinsale is a colourful little town with a fine harbour, and is well worth exploring. It also has a colourful past. The Battle of Kinsale (1601), when the final battle in the Nine Years War was lost to the English army, might just have changed the whole course of Irish history. The solitary peninsula, called the Old Head, is 6 miles (9.7 km) to the south. The route to the start of the walk crosses the Bandon River, with its castles and creeks, and, at low tide, its mud flats and marsh birds. This is followed by a detour to the tiny village of Sandycove, before arriving at the start of the walk. The Old Head is a quiet place. Little remains of the Celtic settlement or of the many ships that have come to grief on its rocky eastern shore. Today it is the haunt of fishermen, bird watchers and rock climbers. The bird sanctuary is a protected area. The numerous coastal tracks here are well-defined, but it is still sometimes disconcerting to watch the fishermen nonchalantly disappearing over steep grassy slopes towards the sea.

1 *Leave Cork on the N71 road. Turn off left 2 miles (3.2 km) after Ballinhassig village towards Kinsale. Go around the harbour to the left to cross the bridge over the Bandon River. Turn right, then shortly left, and right again for Sandycove. Climb steeply at the end of the village and continue straight on to the Old Head, ignoring turns to the right until the car park is reached on the descent towards the castle gate.*
Walk back up to the signal tower, leaving the road a few paces beyond the fork.

2 *Walk down to the castle and turn left by the side of the keep, returning to the road on its far side.*

3 *Walk on to the ruins of the cottage and circular lighthouses near the headland to the south-east.*

4 *Continue to the present lighthouse at the end of the road. Return to the car park by the same route.*

A This signal tower was built in Napoleonic times, to give warning of enemy activity.

B Opposite the car park, the cliff is a bird sanctuary and a breeding ground for many species of sea birds.

C Not a great deal remains of the de Courcy castle, but it makes a splendid entry point at the scraggy neck of the Old Head. There is evidence of much earlier earthworks on either side of the entrance gate. Occupation of the castle ceased in 1587.

D The cottage lighthouse, built in the 17th century, had an opening in the roof for the container on which the fire was kept burning. The circular lighthouse replaced the cottage lighthouse in the 18th century, and is a solid structure with good accommodation nearby for the keepers. It was abandoned in 1853 for the present one, in a more prominent position at the tip of the peninsula.

E The steep cliffs north-west of the lighthouse form another good bird sanctuary. Near here in 1892 the ship *City of Chicago* impaled itself on a rock in thick fog and foundered. Many survived thanks in part to the efforts of the coastguards, who lived in the now ruined building by the road. Those in the *Lusitania*, which was torpedoed 9 miles (14.5 km) to the south in 1915, fared less well.

BARTHOLOMEW WALKS SERIES

Designed to meet the requirements of both experienced and inexperienced walkers, the guides in this series are ideal for anyone who enjoys exploring on foot. They describe the best routes across our greatest walking country from Inverness to the New Forest and Cork & Kerry.

● In each guide, there are at least 30 carefully chosen, easy-to-follow walks over rights of way, with detailed route descriptions accompanying special maps.

● Country walks are graded according to distance and terrain and start from a convenient parking area. The route always returns to the car park, usually by a circular walk and, where appropriate, access by public transport is also possible.

● Notes on local history, geography and wildlife add interest to the walks and the unique notebook format is especially easy to use.

EXPLORE THE BROADS
0 7028 0772 9   £3·50

WALK CORK & KERRY
0 7028 0949 7   £4·95

WALK THE CORNISH COASTAL PATH
A special format step-by-step guide to the entire length of the Cornish Coastal Path (Marsland Mouth - Cremyll).
0 7028 0902 0   £4·95

WALK THE COTSWOLDS
0 7028 0908 X   £4·95

WALK THE DALES
0 7028 0800 8   £4·95

MORE WALKS IN THE DALES
0 7028 0948 9   £4·95

YORKSHIRE DALES VISITOR'S PACK
Containing a copy of *Walk the Dales* and a folded 1 inch map of the Yorkshire Dales in a clear, plastic carrying wallet.
0 7028 0932 2   £6·95

WALK DARTMOOR
0 7028 0688 9   £3·95

WALK DORSET & HARDY'S WESSEX
0 7028 0906 3   £3·95

WALK EXMOOR & THE QUANTOCKS
0 7028 0910 1   £3·95

WALK HERTS & BUCKS
0 7028 0953 5   £4·95

WALK THE LAKES
0 7028 8111 2   £3·95

MORE WALKS IN THE LAKES
0 7028 0819 9   £4·95

LAKE DISTRICT WALKING PACK
Containing a copy of *Walk the Lakes* and a folded 1 inch map of the Lake District in a clear, plastic carrying wallet.
0 7028 0876 8   £6·95

WALK LOCH LOMOND & THE TROSSACHS
0 7028 0744 3   £4·95

WALK LOCH NESS & THE RIVER SPEY
0 7028 0787 7   £3·95

BARTHOLOMEW WALKS SERIES (Contd)

WALK THE PEAK DISTRICT
0 7028 0710 9   £4·95

MORE WALKS IN THE PEAK DISTRICT
0 7028 0951 9   £4·95

WALK PERTHSHIRE
0 7028 0766 4   £3·95

**WALK ROYAL DEESIDE
& NORTH EAST SCOTLAND**
0 7028 0898 9   £3·95

WALK LONDON
0 7028 0771 0   £3·95

WALK SNOWDONIA & NORTH WALES
0 7028 0804 0   £3·95

WALK LOTHIAN, THE BORDERS & FIFE
0 7028 0803 2   £3·95

WALK THE SOUTH DOWNS
0 7028 0811 3   £3·95

WALK THE NEW FOREST
0 7028 0810 5   £4·95

WALK THE SOUTH PENNINES
0 7028 0955 1   £4·95

WALK THE NORTH DOWNS
0 7028 0742 7   £3·95

**WALK SOUTH WALES
& THE WYE VALLEY**
0 7028 0904 7   £3·95

WALK THE NORTH YORK MOORS
0 7028 0743 5   £3·95

WALK NORTHUMBRIA
0 7028 0959 4   £4·95

WALK SOUTH WEST SCOTLAND
0 7028 0900 4   £3·95

WALK OBAN, MULL & LOCHABER
0 7028 0801 6   £3·95

WALK THE THAMES & CHILTERNS
0 7028 0802 4   £3·95

- -

Guides in this series may be purchased from good bookshops. In the event of difficulty copies may be obtained by post.
Please send your order with your remittance to
**BARTHOLOMEW BOOKSERVICE BY POST,
PO BOX 29, DOUGLAS, ISLE OF MAN, BRITISH ISLES.**

NAME

ADDRESS

Please enclose a cheque or postal order made out to 'Bartholomew' for the amount due and allow 25 pence per book postage & packing fee up to a maximum of £3.00.
While every effort is made to keep prices low, it is sometimes necessary to increase cover prices at short notice.
Bartholomew reserves the right to show new retail prices on covers which may differ from those previously advertised in the text or elsewhere.